Undivided Love

Courtland Jerome Akers Jr

CHAPTER FIVE
Love Making

CHAPTER SIX
Love her So

CHAPTER SEVEN
Life or Death

CHAPTER EIGHT
Built to Last

THANK YOU JESUS!

All Glory goes to God. This book was inspired by God to give a better understanding of his Word concerning Marriage. It is not from a personal perspective or experience. However, it totally focuses on God's design for marriage, which from the beginning was built to last. So, as Apostle Paul said,

But I certify you, brethren that the gospel which was preached of me is not after man. For I neither received it of man, neither was I taught it, but by the revelation Jesus Christ (Galatians 1:12)

CHAPTER ONE

Undivided Love

1

UNDIVIDED LOVE

THEREFORE SHALL A MAN LEAVE HIS FATHER AND HIS MOTHER AND <u>CLEAVE</u> UNTO HIS WIFE. (GENESIS 2:24)

Marriage is the most beautiful relationship that a man can experience with a woman when it's operating in accordance to God's definition of it. Since the beginning marriage was built to last forever; therefore, divorce wasn't a part of God's original plan. He blessed Adam and Eve and ordered them to bring forth the good fruits of life. He commanded them to make love, fill the earth, and to reign over all things. For all power was in their hands. He wanted them to eat the fruits of Love, Joy, Peace, Temperance, Faith, Goodness, Gentleness, Longsuffering, and Meekness from one another. He created them in his image which is righteousness and true holiness; therefore, they would have naturally brought forth fruits unto God and loved one another the way he intended for them to. Marriage was designed to be a sweet and pleasant everlasting relationship sharing a love that couldn't be divided. Marriage was never meant to be a snare. Neither was it meant to be a trap for abuse, sorrow, or shame. Due to Adam's disobedience, sin entered into the world, and corrupted the minds of man, which has caused many marriages to be unfruitful.

To this day many fear marriage for different reasons. Some of the reasons are: the fear of commitment, the fear of betrayal, the fear of divorce, the fear of being unhappy, the fear of becoming bored with the same sex partner for the duration of your life and the fear of experiencing the horrors that took place in others people's marriage. These fears keep many running away from holy matrimony, but two people who really love God will love one another the way they should, and the spirit of fear will find no place to rest in them, because perfect love casts out all fear. When you give your heart completely to God, trust and exercise his Word, you will walk in the confidence of knowing that God

7

won't allow you to encounter anything that you couldn't handle. There will never be a need to fear anything he allows to test your marriage.

In order for marriages to be successful, husbands and wives must obey the Gospel of Jesus Christ. For Christ is the head of every man; therefore, at the time of life when a boy becomes a man, and gets married he must leave his parents covering and submit to the Lordship of Jesus Christ. Though he should always honor his parents they no longer regulate him. Christ has complete control of that man and his wife, and they must labor to build their own house together in My Lord. Neither the man nor his wife is self-willed. They must do the will of God even if their parents do not agree. Jesus was subject to his parent's authority until God the Father took control of him. At that point, He left his parent's covering, manifested His glory, and began to build the Church, his only concern was the will of God. He gave us an example of how a man should love his wife. He cleaved unto His bride: He fought, suffered, prayed, and died for the Church. His love was tested constantly and regardless of how difficult the test was, He remained obedient to the will of God at the expense of his life. Yet, in laying down his life he saved his wife. For that's a mark of tried and true love. He denied himself the life of sinful pleasures, worldly riches and bore his cross being a blessing to his Church. He redeemed his wife with his blood and washed her with His Word.

My Lord commands a man to cleave to his wife as He did his Church. Cleave means to stay with and stick closely to; therefore, when a man cleaves to his woman, he is becoming exclusively intimate to every part of her body, mind, soul, and spirit. They shall become perfectly joined together having no divisions between them. The enemy hates to see a man closely knitted to his woman. When a man and his woman are close it's difficult to tear them apart. That closeness is accomplished through love,

8

honest communication, faithfulness, etc. When the light shines in a marriage, God is being glorified in it and thus Satan does what he can to put the light out. All of hell will attempt to rip them apart, shake them apart, cut them apart, pry them apart, and pull them apart, but as long as they obey God nothing will be able divide them. A man must cleave to his woman through every trial, tribulation, and unexpected situations. He can't let her go when the lines are thick nor when the lines become thin. He must hold on to her firmly, and they must maintain their loyalty to one another during the storms of life. For as long as they live, they should be inseparable. Nothing should come before thy soul mate, but the will of My Lord and His will is that they let nothing cut them asunder.

Notice in the beginning when God created Adam and Eve, he created them male and female. They were husband and wife. He did not create them with earthly parents, siblings, or with children. God gave them time together without any interference. For he made them one flesh, he did not make them to be one with their parents, siblings, friends, or one with their children, but one with one another, and for that cause should a man leave his father mother, and cleave unto his wife. Nothing should divide them into two because they are one. This shows the importance of the husband and wife relationship. They need to be each other's main priority. It's God's will that they value their relationship with one another more than anything other than Him. They should never let family, friends, the club, sports, money, or children come in between them.

Many people weren't driven by wisdom into marriage, but their LUST to be married took them down a road called misery lane. Since lust was the foundation of their marriage it made it easy for the enemy to divide and conquer them. One of the differences between being driven by lust and being guided by wisdom is that wisdom won't lead you to marry someone you neither understand nor can communicate with. Neither will it instruct you to marry someone on the hope that they will change nor to marry someone who acts as though he or she doesn't care about you, but LUST will. Lust is only concerned about such things as, how good you look, how much money you make, or what it can USE you for. Who can be truly happy in their marriage, if they're married to someone that doesn't care about them? In order to build a lasting marriage husbands and wives should get into each other's affairs, and show one another that they care, because when you love someone you will be concerned about the issues of their heart. Trust can never be established in the relationship of those who don't commune, understand, or care about one another.

Couples should always keep a positive and joyful attitude knowing that the enemy hates the light that shines in their sweet union. It causes them great discomfort to witness happiness being shared amongst you the one you love. When they see you two having a good time in each other's presence it makes them sick to their stomach. The thought of you being loving and affectionate with one another torments their mind. Understand the enemy wishes he was in thy shoes, and since he doesn't have it for himself, he doesn't want you with it. His only means of obtaining any joy is by taken it from you; therefore, don't let the devil rob you of it. For this reason he does his best to sow discord in between you two, aiming to destroy everything that you've worked together to establish. When you're stressed out, complaining, bitter and miserable with one another, your enemies are clapping their hands and high fiving each other. When your fight and warring against one another your enemies are placing bets on who shall win. Understand, Satan's primary concern is to prevent you from bringing forth the fruits of the Spirit because then and only then is God glorified in you. He doesn't want your relationship full of Love, Goodness, Peace, etc. You should always do those things that would produce the good fruits of life, and stand strong in faith against the envious that put in work trying to break down what My Lord has purposed built to last.

Always rejoice when people persecute your marriage because your reward shall be great in the Kingdom. It angers the enemy when you count it all joy concerning your trials. Never do thy enemies' will by letting go of the one My Lord has bonded you with, but increase his hatred by growing closer to one another. The woman is a weaker vessel, and she needs her man to be strong when the pressure builds. His strength will be needed to keep her close when storms occur. He must hold her tight when the storm blows violent winds of adversity, jealousy, envy, strife, confusion, lies, and all sorts of hell their way in hopes to blow both of them in different directions. They must always pray and obey My Lord who is able to keep them from falling.

BLESSED MARRIAGE

Many Couples are not happy together because they are living the life that Adam and Eve lived after God punished them for disobeying him. The fruit of sin has been brought forth in their marriage which is sorrow. Till this day we have husbands pointing all the blame on the woman, the woman pointing the blame at the devil and no one is acknowledging their part. That isn't the life God purposed for them to live; therefore, to understand what God intended for marriage, we must study what life was life before they disobeyed God and sin entered in, because that's the Life they would have lived forever in the presence of God had they not sinned.

Genesis 1:28 And God blessed them, and God said unto them, be fruitful, and multiply, and replenish the earth, and subdue it: and have dominion over the fish of the sea, and over the fowl of the air, and over every living thing that moveth upon the earth.

HE BLESSED THEM

The first thing God did to Adam and Eve was Bless them. The Blessings of God maketh rich and he adds no sorrow to it, so their marriage was destined to prosper and flourish into a beautiful vine of love and happiness. They would have been spending all their days together in the presence of God having gladness of heart. His seal of approval was on their marriage.

BE FRUITFUL

Galatians 5:22 But THE FRUIT of the Spirit is love, joy, peace, longsuffering, gentleness, goodness, faith, 23 Meekness, temperance: against such there is no law.
1. LOVE

2. JOY
3. PEACE
4. LONGSUFFERING
5. GENTLENESS
6. GOODNESS
7. FAITH
8. MEEKNESS
9. TEMPERANCE

It was The Lord's will for Adam and Eve to bring forth fruit within them so that they walk in the abundance of life, but that fruit could only be brought forth through obedience to his Voice. Christ is the Voice of God and it's impossible for men and women to bear good fruits without him, but those who believe and hearken to the Words of Christ do bring forth those good fruits.

John 15:5 I am the vine, ye are the branches: He that abideth in me, and I in him, the same bringeth forth much fruit: for without ME ye can do nothing.

Men and women examine yourselves because if you don't have love, joy, peace, etc. within yourself, it doesn't matter how much you bring to the table, your spouse can't enjoy what's on the table because your hateful, troubled, depressed, mean-spirited self is sitting at the table. Men you may be providing a nice house, but if you don't bear good fruits your wife wont like living in that nice house with you. Wives you may be sexy and domesticated, but if you don't bear good fruit your husband wont desire your arrogant, rebellious, unsweetened self; therefore, men and women if you want a beautiful relationship abide in Christ and bring forth good fruit.

MULTIPLY YOUR FRUIT

Matthew 13:3 And he spake many things unto them in parables, saying, Behold, a sower went forth to sow;

Matthew 13:23 But he that received seed into the good ground is he that heareth the word, and understandeth it; which also beareth fruit, and bringeth forth, some an hundredfold, some sixty, some thirty.

God's desire is for us to grow continuously in the love, peace, joy, etc. of his Spirit, which comes through keeping and understanding his WORD. Overtime as long as a man and his wife continue to walk in Christ everything should get better for them. Their love should deepen, their peace shall be greater, and their joy shall be fuller. While everyone else is falling apart your marriage will feel as though it's being renewed day by day because you're not doing anything to cause your fruit to wither away.

Jn. 15:16 Ye have not chosen me, but I have chosen you, and ordained you, that ye should go and bring →forth fruit,← and that your fruit should remain: that whatsoever ye shall ask of the Father in my name, he may give it you.

REPLENISH

GOD commanded man to replenish the earth meaning populate it, which requires for married couples to have sex and bear children. It was God's desire for earth to be filled with godly people. This is why it's important to bring forth good fruit that you may produce godly seed. According to the Word the more children you have the merrier.

Psalms 127:3-5 Lo, children are a heritage of the LORD: and the fruit of the womb is his reward.4 As arrows are in the hand of a mighty man; so are children of the youth.5 Happy is the man that hath his quiver full of →them:← they shall not be ashamed, but they shall speak with the enemies in the gate.

SUBDUE IT

God commanded Adam and Eve to subdue the earth meaning to bring everything under subjection. As married couples you must establish order for things in your life. Everything that's in your path or that's out of control you must subdue it. GOD has blessed you with everything you need to CONQUER your enemies.

Romans 8:37 Nay, in all these things we are more than conquerors through him that loved us.

DOMINION

Dominion means to rule, dominate or tread down. God gave Adam and Eve dominion over everything that moved upon the earth, so they were the most powerful entity of all living creatures upon the earth. Husbands and reigns walking in Christ should reign over every area in their life. This world is yours for the taking. Don't allow nothing or no one to stand in your way. Anything that's ruling over you such as money, kids, health, pets, etc. is because you allow it to. In Christ everything in the world must fall under your feet.

Luke 10:19 Behold, I give unto power to tread on serpents and scorpions, and over all the power of the enemy: and nothing by any means shall hurt you. 20 Notwithstanding in this rejoice not, that the spirits are subject unto you; but rather rejoice, that your names are written in heaven.

MARITAL VOWS

(The Traditional Vows)
I TAKE YOU TO BE MY LAWFULLY WEDDED HUSBAND/WIFE TO
HAVE AND TO HOLD FROM THIS DAY FORWARD FOR BETTER,
FOR WORSE, FOR RICHER, FOR POORER, IN SICKNESS AND IN
HEALTH UNTIL DEATH DO US PART!

If you recited vows at your wedding ceremony acknowledge every word that you spoke because your vows are an oath that you made under the witness of God to love and cleave to one another. Those vows shall be thoroughly tested, so if you didn't seriously mean those words you should have never spoken those words. Marriage is not a game, by the behavior of many you would think it was, because after making those vows they jumped in and out of marriage like they were playing hopscotch. You may have been talking to fast when you made that vow, but God take those VOWS you made very seriously, so lay it to heart that the Oath you made before him you are required to keep it for the duration of life. Don't ever make a promise you can't fulfill. When you make a vow and tell someone that you love them, if your heart is sincere, then nothing should be able to separate your love from them. Regardless of the situation, trial, or test that they face, your love for them should endure through it all. Many confess love at the altar but when adversity arises they fall away quick. After the storm arrives their attitude takes a 180 degree turn and now they can't stand being around you. They feel that you're not worth the hassle that they have to go through to be with you. The loyalty of their love was tested and it failed.

Don't vow for better, for worse if you know that if the sun stop shining in your marriage you'll become an Olympic track star and sprint out of your marriage. Don't vow for richer, for poorer and as soon as your spouse lose his/her job and isn't able to find immediate employment or is forced to take job with much lesser pay, you become a magician and perform a disappearing act. Don't vow in sickness and in health and as soon as your spouse is diagnosed with a life threatening or debilitating illness, you become as a fugitive and break free. Don't vow until death do you part and after a short span of time. you become an alarm clock and start sounding off TIMES UP because you're tired of being married. Don't vow anything you can't live up to and certainly don't say you made a mistake marrying him or her. You knew who you were marrying before you said I do, and if you didn't know who you marrying then shame on you to make a vow to cleave to a stranger. It's better to never get married than to make vow and not be true to it. Understand that God is not playing with you. He's holding you accountable for every word you speak, so be true to your Word.

When thou vowest a vow unto God, defer not to pay it; for he hath no pleasure in fools: pay that which thou hast vowed. Better is it that thou shouldest not vow, than that thou shouldest vow and not pay. Suffer not thy mouth to cause thy flesh to sin; neither say thou before the angel, that it was an error: wherefore should God be angry at thy voice, and destroy the work of thine hands? (Ecclesiastes 5:4)

Never make a vow to God that you're not going to be true to, because if you stop honoring that vow, you sin against God and he shall punish you. When a marriage falls apart, it reveals either one or both the husband and wife was flattering one another when they made those vows at the altar. Had they been sincere how could it end? Real love never dies, but instead, it develops and grows stronger. Over time you learn to love each other better seeing that your hearts are sealed as one. All marriages go through seasons and stages of development. During the night season the relationship goes through a series of tests. It's a difficult period, however, if the love of Christ is the spirit that's melting your hearts together, thou shall overcome all things. You will consistently grow through the storms, afflictions, and persecutions. For the Love of Christ endures through every sickness, every tragedy, every struggle, every issue, and any other dart of the wicked one. Though weeping endureth through the night, joy cometh in the morning; therefore, hang on to one another in troubled times and don't let time tick you out. Endure the storm and always be compassionate with each other. Demonstrate Love in-spite of the weather. My Lord will see you through thy situations and fill your heart with gladness. Be thankful unto Him and bless His Holy Name. Great peace shall manifest in the marriage of those that stuck it out through the storm. Joy shall consume their heart and their scars shall be a testimony of their undying love. Husbands and wives that stay true to the WORD of God establish a long history of good memories together. They can proclaim how they stand upon the Rock and how when the storm came and the winds blew they fell not, because love is their everlasting foundation. Their marriage will be a living testimony of what My Lord can do, if you continue to stay true to your WORD.

REAL LOVE

Husbands and wives need to exhibit real love to one another because when someone truly loves you, their love for you comes without an expiration date. They will never abandon you and in times of storm their love is even made more evident to you, showing you they won't allow anything to separate them from you. The only way you can lose their Love is to walk away from it and in walking away from it you will be forsaking your own goodness and mercy. Understand, ONLY a fool walks away from love; therefore, don't become one knowing as long as you don't depart from their love their Love will never be taken away from you. It's a love worth fighting for because real love

Beareth all things, believeth all things, hopeth all things, endureth all things.(1 Corinthians 13:7)

When you marry someone it should be for love. Love is the most powerful entity alive and imaginable. Love is everything God is, so to know what love is, is to know Him. It is an Action Word that displays his goodness, his mercies, and his righteousness. Oh so often, love is only verbally expressed, but there is not any truth or strength in those words if love isn't being physically expressed. Love is a Spirit that every born again believer possesses and is commanded to walk in. It is a way of life and that life is Christ which is a Heavenly One. The Love of Christ will never fail thee nor forsake thee. Regardless of how long the storm lasts, His love will be there, unlike others, if the storm doesn't calm quickly, they'll run out of your life. If your situation doesn't change when or before they expect it to, they'll depart from you. They were too weak to hold on because if they truly had loved thee with the Love of Christ, their love would not have left you. There is nothing too strong or too long that can prevent real love from holding on. The Love of Christ will outlast any and everything. His love is eternal; therefore, it never grows weary, weak, or tired of loving.

Husbands and wives, how can you tell your spouse you love them, but when all hell breaks loose in their life, you walk away from him or her? If your Love is real your love won't cease for them when trouble starts, but those that do walk away, it wasn't love keeping them there in the first place. If they valued the things they did with their spouse more than their spouse, for whatever reason if their spouse cease from doing those things with them, they'll become impatient and seek another to enjoy those things with. Those Things could include sex, partying, traveling, sports, drinking, drugs, etc. The Love of Christ is patient, so if the love of Christ abides in them, they'll be patient as well. However, if their love evaporates in the storm they did not sincerely love you.

Couples must also remember when you have a good husband or wife many are going to lust for them. You will have to fight the enemy tooth and nail because when devils see that you have something good, they want to steal it from you. Knowing this, should make a man and/or woman be on their P's and Q's, seeing that they have someone that many dream about. Love thou spouse better than anyone else and endure through every struggle. Many have the attitude that they shouldn't have to fight for their man or woman, so they will literally sit back and watch the devil as he takes what belongs to them. This is what happens when someone else acknowledges their worth and you don't.

IF THOU FAINT IN THE DAY OF ADVERSITY, THY STRENGTH IS SMALL (PROVERBS 24:10)

Every marriage is going to be met with adversity. Satan is going to throw every dart possible to sever what My Lord has put together. Therefore, in order to handle the onslaughts of the enemy, couples must be armed with the whole armor of God. The Shield of Faith is needed to stand against the wiles of the devil. They must dwell together in the bond of peace and be strapped with the Word of God because the closer two people become and the more knowledge of God they possess, the stronger they are. Trials will come to test their strength and in that day of confrontation, if they began to fall apart, they weren't strong at all. Though they thought they loved each other, their love was with hypocrisy, which is un-perfected love. Couples can feel they love each other in heart. but until a person comes to know God through My Lord and Savior Jesus Christ, they don't even know what love is.

The weak can't handle opposition and can't endure the race. The trial is too hot for them. Therefore, they don't last long. The enemy gets into their mind quickly, causing them to wax weak and faint. As soon as trouble begins, a weak person turns bitter and begins to wither. They weren't able to stand in the face of jealousy, envy, lies, nor hatred. Persecution offended them and snatched the seed out of their hearts and became unforgiving, unmerciful, etc. They allowed the enemy to come in and cut them asunder. However, when two people walk in the Love of God, they walk in strength and can stand against anything. For everything the enemy does to quench their love, becomes the fuel they need to love each other more intensely.

MANY WATERS CAN'T QUENCH LOVE. (SONGS 8:7)

Regardless of the financial issues, insecurity issues, health issues, or whatever issues the waters attempt to flood into thy marriage, if two people are strong, it won't quench the flame of their love, but it shall burn more. For no one will be able to say or do anything that would prevent their love from growing stronger. In the end, they will see and deeply appreciate what love has brought them through. They'll have a history of triumph and a long life together. Love strengthens; it is as strong as death. It destroys the will of your enemies. Everything that's in the way must move out of the way, and everything that rises up against thee will fall by thy wayside. For when couples truly love, their bond is so strong, that nothing can break them. However, couples that are despising one another weaken their relationship and as a result, the enemies' desire usually gets accomplished in them, because weak relationships can't persevere through trials. They are liable to fall apart the day Satan spreads one lie. The weak can be easily broken in a struggle. A storm tests the foundation and strength of a relationship. Immediately when the unwise get tried, they turn on one another and quickly become foes. However, those that are weak in Christ, if they hold on to the faith, their strength should be made perfect in weakness.

Many couples lived in lust before marriage and never learned how to love each other. Their lust deceived them to believe that they loved each other, but once they got married their eyes were opened. They despised each other in heart. When you're not walking in the Love of Christ, you're walking in the lust of the flesh and fleshly love is a love that stands next to a thin line across from hate. If the person that declares how much they love you and wants to take care of your heart, is the same person who screams they hate you and does things to offend you when a disagreement arises, that person doesn't love thee. They were walking time bombs, wolves in sheep's clothing that only you with their words. Their love exploded in thy face in the day of adversity, because they weren't real. The weak freeze up at the sound of struggles. They give more value to the problem than the relationship. They don't feel their spouse is worth putting in the extra effort to hold on to. Have you ever heard someone say that it's not worth all of that? They confess to love you but they don't want to pay their price. They say they love you but they won't fight, pray, nor persevere through the storm for you. They were hypocrites!

How would you know a person loves you until they got tested? For example, let's say a successful man who has an excellent job making over six figures a year, with excellent benefits, gets married. However, within two years his company downsizes and lays him off. The lifestyle he was use to living, he can no longer uphold until he finds himself another high paying position. Let's assume he doesn't find a job immediately in his field and he's forced to sell his property, trade in his car, and takes a blue collar job. His mood might not be the greatest because of his situation. If his wife is a weak woman, instead of being understanding, encouraging, and compassionate towards him, she will make him feel worse about it. She's frustrated because she can't do what she is accustomed to doing, so she begins to make him feel as though he's not worth the struggle. She had no problems putting up with his moods before, but now that he's struggling to maintain, she can't handle his mood any longer, suddenly it becomes too much for her, isn't that strange? Now she talks to him any kind of way. Now she calls him weak, now he's not a man to her nor can he do anything for her. She can no longer brag about his position and since she doesn't value the man that he is, she finds it unnecessary to remain married to him. She only loved and respected his money, and now since that appears to be gone, she quickly runs out of his life. She doesn't have the faith nor does she want the faith to know that God shall supply all of their needs according to His riches and glory. He found the woman he gave the honor's wasn't even his friend when the storm arose.

A woman who is strong won't move, she will stand by her man, and won't allow any devil in hell to turn her love and respect away from the one whom My Lord has joined her with. She'll be more understanding of his moods and she will encourage and strengthen him in the time of storm. His presence is more valuable to her than his money, and she will do all in her power to help him endure the storm. Couples walking in the strength of love won't let an outsider or situation come in and disrupt their relationship. Couples must be strong and confront their problems head on. They must be able to take a blow with a smile and continue to do the will of My Lord knowing that He can and that He will avenge the enemy and make a way out of no way. Godly marriages are built to last and they will breathe life continuously. They cannot be moved. Their LOVE brings forth the everlasting fruits of righteousness, giving My Lord glory. It is a token of hope breathing life into many dead relationships. They'll be a blessing to many. However, many marriages end, not because the problem was too big to handle, but they were too weak to stand. They had neither faith nor any patience to wait on God.

MARRIAGE IS FOR LIFE

They say unto him, Why did Moses them command to give a writing of divorcement, and put her away? He saith unto them, Moses because of the hardness of your hearts suffered you to put away your wives: but from the beginning it was not so. (Matthew 19:7,8)

Moses redefined Marriage by adding the precept of divorce for any reason to it, being that once sin entered the world and corrupted the ways of men, men and women began to ill treat one another and they looked for any reason to get out of marriage quicker than they did for getting married. Christ set the record straight when he said from the beginning **IT WAS NOT SO;** therefore, he taught that divorce wasn't a part of God's original plan for man, but that Moses wrote that precept because of the hardness of man's heart. God allowed divorce to become an option because many aren't true to their marriage vows nor do God put all marriages together. Example, Now that homosexuality has greatly increased the government has taken steps to redefine God's definition of Marriage by legalizing same sex marriage. This step by legislature is PROOF that God doesn't put all marriages together because there is no way on this earth God is going to put two males or two females together. God didn't make another male to be the glory and help meet of the man. He made Adam one woman which was Eve, so only a female can be a man's wife.

Matthew 19:5,6 Have you not read, that he which made them at the beginning made them a male and female, and said, For this cause shall a man leave his father and mother and shall cleave unto his wife: and they twain shall be one flesh?

God is not the author of confusion. Same sex couples cannot become ONE FLESH. God does not put same sexes together because they would be unable to obey the Will of God which is to be fruitful and multiply! It's impossible for SAME SEX couples to have SEX because they're not equipped with appropriate body parts to become one body. What they do is not considered to be sex in God's eyes. but it's rightfully called VILE AFFECTIONS. Homosexuality and bestiality an unnatural act and takes one of a depraved mind to indulge in such horrendous practices. The Law of man changes, but the Law of God doesn't change nor does Man have the power to change his Law. As a believer you must decide who you're going to serve. Although can be politically correct you still can be biblically wrong, so either you can be governed by the laws of man or be governed by the Word of God. It was never God's will nor will it ever be His will for same genders to have sexual relations. Although man may honor it, He doesn't honor it because it's detestable to him.

Leviticus 18:22 Thou shalt not lie with mankind, as with womankind: it is abomination.

Leviticus 20:13 If a man also lie with mankind, as he lieth with a woman, both of them have committed an abomination: they shall surely be put to death; their blood shall be upon them.

Those who call themselves believers of Christ, but support the right for homosexuals to marry make the commandments of God of none effect! You cannot be a follower of Christ and stand in support of things that go against the doctrines of Christ. Regardless of how popular and widespread homosexuality has become, God doesn't change his mind. Wrong is Wrong regardless if the world say it's right. The Disciples of Christ teaches us that homosexuality goes against nature itself.

Romans 1: 26,27, 32 For this cause God gave them up unto vile affections: for even their women did change the natural use into that which is against nature: 27 and likewise also the men, leaving the natural use of the woman, burned in their lust one toward another; men with men working that which is unseemly, and

receiving in themselves that recompense of their error which is meet.

32 Who knowing the judgment of God, that they which commit such things are →worthy of death←, not only do the same, but have pleasure in them that do them.

Homosexuality is a death worthy act. Again, it is impossible for same sexes to become one. When God joins a male and a female together they are no more Twain but One Flesh. They are not TWO separate and single individuals, but they are bound together being One Body till death separates them. When you're bound together you're not free to marry anyone else.

Women don't let a man deceive you with scriptures saying that it's acceptable for a man to have more than one wife! Under the Mosaic Law a man was allowed to have multiple wives, but in Christ we are UNDER A NEW TESTAMENT in which Christ is the messenger of that covenant and we receive the law at his mouth. According to the doctrine of Christ, men cannot have more than one wife because they are not Free. Men that marry more than one woman are called ADULTERERS just as women who marry more than one man are Adulteress. Paul teaches us this principle

Romans 7:2-3 For the woman which hath an →husband is bound by the law to her husband so long as he liveth; but if the husband be dead,← she→is loosed from the law of her husband. So then if, while her husband liveth, she be married to another man, she shall be called an adulteress: but if her husband be dead, she is →free←from that law; so that she is no adulteress, though she be married to another man.

Only through death or fornication is man or woman loosed from the law of their spouse and free to marry someone else.

WHEREFORE THEY ARE NO LONGER TWAIN BUT ONE FLESH. WHAT

26

THEREFORE GOD HATH JOINED TOGETHER LET NO MAN PUT ASUNDER. (MATTHEW 19:6)

Understand there is war against your marriage and the command is to let no man put asunder what The Heavenly Father has consolidated. This is a defensive strategy because God knows the enemy is going to try his best to break you two apart. Always be on guard because the enemy is constantly looking for ways to get in your marriage, because many problems that arise in marriages are because of what couples have LET into their marriage. Together you are a packed power house and with the shield of faith, you have all you need to keep your enemies out. They can't do anything more than what you "LET" them do. As long as you don't LET them in your marriage their dreams can never come true. Don't let them counsel you, don't let them seduce you, don't let them touch you and if you don't let them do those things, their only wasting their time fighting you.

Why do the heathen rage and the people imagine a vain thing for the kings of this earth and the ruler take counsel together against the Lord and his anointed, saying, →LET US BREAK THEIR BANDS ASUNDER← (PSALM 2:1)

Let's dig deeper into the mindset of the enemy, but first let's be reminded that the instruction given to husbands and wives were to let no man put them asunder, but notice that the enemy is saying, "Let us break their bands asunder." This reveals that the enemies' will for your marriage is the exact opposite of Gods will for your marriage. God's will is for your marriage to last, but Satan's will is for your marriage to end in divorce. Imagine Satan and his team of demons holding a conference meeting to figure out ways to enter and cause havoc in your relationship. They frequently form a huddle and discuss their plan of attack. They have been assigned to trouble your marriage by any means necessary. They'll use internet, ex-lovers, porn, money, beauty, family, etc. to come in between you two. They will use whoever makes themselves available to them to war against your marriage. Your enemies are envious of you and they hate the thought of you being happy together. Every time you enter their presence you can clearly see the hate in some of their faces. Some of them will intentionally laugh loudly, utter or whisper things in hopes of crawling into your mind and causing you to make false assumptions that could lead you to falsely accuse or interrogate your spouse with such questions as: 1. Do you know them? 2. Did you use to talk or be involved with one of them? 3. If not, then why are they looking at us like that? 4. Why are they whispering to each other as though they know you? 5. Why did he/she make that comment? 6. You must have slept with or is sleeping with one of them." On the other side of the coin of hate, many are silently despising your marriage. They are the one's smiling in your face while talking badly behind your back. They take things you say out of context and/or twist them and then go spread nasty rumors and lies in attempts to divide your love, so it's important for couples to not be ignorant of Satan's devices which have torn many asunder.

Your marriage is sure to be tested, so handle every situation wisely as they come. The only reason your enemies are showing out is in hopes to get into your mind and cause confusion, but reverse the madness by doing the exact of opposite of what they want you to do. Every time they make a move to sever you apart draw closer to one another. Every time they whisper or make funny faces don't try to decode what their facial expression mean, but rather pay them no attention and kiss one another. No matter what never do their will. Couples must always remember that the enemy forms weapons to ruin thy marriage and they are glad when wars take place in it. However, happy are those who stand on the Word of God because no weapon formed against them will succeed. There is nothing currently in existence nor can be created that's strong enough to destroy your marriage. Those who God has put together, He wants them to stay together. He has placed his seal of love on them and now it's up to them to make sure they let nothing stop them from loving one another. As long as couples love one another the way they are supposed to, what can go wrong? My Lord has promised that he wouldn't allow you to face anything that you couldn't bear, so however he allows your relationship to be tested, the test itself is to help perfect your love for one another. However, If thou don't endure the process, the same test that could have strengthen your marriage will destroy it.

CLOSER LOOK AT ADULTERY

What therefore God hath joined together, let not man put asunder.10 And in the house his disciples asked him again of the same matter. 11 And he saith unto them, Whosoever shall put away his wife,←AND—marry another, →committeth adultery← against her. 12 And if a woman shall put away her husband, and be married to another, she committeth adultery. (Mark 10:9-12)

When we look at these passages of scriptures closely, Christ is giving us volumes of wisdom in a few words. It teaches us that Judges and/or the Court System doesn't have the power to break asunder what God has joined together. Therefore, though a man or woman gets a divorce on paper that doesn't necessarily mean your divorced in God's eyes because no man can put asunder What God joined together. If God truly joined you two together, only God can break you two asunder.

Notice in the scripture above that if either the man or the woman divorced their spouses and MARRIED someone else they have committed adultery against each other. Also notice, Adultery wasn't committed until they MARRIED someone else. This Law applied to both the woman and the man, so this doctrine eliminates the belief that a man can have more than one wife, because if a man could have more than one wife, he wouldn't be committing adultery against his ex-wife by marrying another woman.

It hath been said, Whosoever shall put away his wife, let him give her a writing of divorcement: 32 But I say unto you, That whosoever shall put away his wife, —saving for the cause of fornication,←→ causeth her to commit adultery: and whosoever shall marry her that is→divorced committeth adultery.←(Matthew 5:31)

Let me re-emphasize getting a divorce in the Court System doesn't mean you're divorced in God's eyes. If you divorce your spouse for the wrong reasons you are only setting yourself up for a trap. As we look at the passage of scriptures above we see that if a man married a divorced woman he committed adultery. How can marrying a —divorced woman←be committing adultery unless in Gods eyes the divorced woman was still married? Again, Paul gives us a thorough teaching on this

Know ye not, brethren, (for I speak to them that know the law,) how that the law hath dominion over a man —as long as he liveth?← 2 For the woman which hath an husband is bound by the law to her husband so long as he liveth; but→if the husband be dead, ←she is loosed from the law of her husband. 3 So then if, while her husband liveth, she be —married to another man←, she shall be called an adulteress:←but if her husband be dead, she —is free←from that law; so that she is no adulteress, though she be married to another man. (Romans 7:1-3)

- **DEATH** of one's spouse is the one of the three things that liberates a man or woman to marry someone else.

- **FORNICATION** is the other cause a man or woman can be liberated from their spouse. If your spouse has sex with someone else you have a right to put him or her away and marry someone else. Weight gain, lost their job, poor health, unhappy, disagreements, mistakes, nerve wrecking, etc. are not reasons to divorce your spouse. Those that divorce for any of those reasons are playing with **Fire** because the day they get →married← to anyone else they commit adultery. As long as your spouse doesn't cross the lines such as infidelity or Abuse, then you need to work out whatever problems you have with them.

- **PHYSICAL ABUSE** is a biblically justifiable reason to divorce because abuse is a solid of expression of hate. Anytime a man or woman is being abused they're literally on death's row because they never know what act of abuse rather intentionally or unintentionally could lead to their fatality. Marriage should be a love experience, but if you're married to an abusive man or woman you're married to a murderer and your marriage shall be a HATE-FILLED experience.

1 John 3:15 Whosoever hateth his brother is a murderer: and ye know that no murderer hath eternal life abiding in him.

In my humblest opinion, if you're married to a Murderer, God will certainly understand if you divorce him or her. Many men and women are responsible for the bloodshed of their spouses. Many children suffer greatly from the loss of their mothers and/or fathers and many parents mourn the loss of their children who were murdered by a Monster. If you're married to someone that claims to love you, but acts hateful pray, pray, pray! God can change them and in some cases he will and other cases it may not be His will for you to remain in it. Some people are avid believers that divorce is never the answer. However, some of those same people would be alive today if they would have taken that way of escape. Again, Christ did teach that there should be no divorce saving the cause of fornication. However, if a man is abusing his wife, then it is clear he has no respect for God or his wife and if he doesn't respect his wife in the house, what makes her think he's respecting her outside the house? If he is that hateful towards her what's stopping him from having an affair? Any man who has the mindset to abuse his wife is a threat to her life and it would be wise of a woman to depart from him or vice versa! It's better to separate from him and stay alive than to remain with him and be killed by him. Don't ever think that God desires for you to remain with a monster, so if the man or woman you're married too, love getting violent with you, understand God hates your spouse.

THE LORD TRIETH THE RIGHTEOUS: BUT THE WICKED AND HIM THAT <u>LOVETH</u> VIOLENCE <u>HIS SOUL HATETH</u>. (PSALM 11:5)

If your married to someone that God hates, you need to really take precaution because many violent men have killed their spouses all because he or she wanted a divorce from. They felt they'd rather see her or him dead before they see them with anyone else. People who are in this situation are in grave danger. They must persevere in prayer and proceed to the exit door with caution. Consider divorce as a way of escape that God has provided for those who have to come the realization that they married a MURDERER

CHAPTER TWO

POWER OF ONE

2

POWER OF ONE

NOW I BESEECH YOU, BRETHREN BY THE NAME OF OUR LORD JESUS CHRIST, THAT YE ALL SPEAK THE SAME THING, AND THAT THERE BE NO DIVISIONS AMONG YOU, BUT THAT YE BE PERFECTLY JOINED TOGETHER IN THE SAME MIND AND IN THE SAME JUDGEMENT. (1CORINTHIANS 1:10)

Apostle Paul, when addressing the Church of God at Corinth, beckoned for the people of God to be as **ONE.**   When two or more people are in the same mind, the same judgment, and speaking the same things, they have become perfectly joined together meaning **One** in the same.   For they are **One,** touching and agreeing on everything.   **One** means perfection.   Couples must strive to become **One.** Oh how sweet it is for the brethren to dwell together in unity. The blessing shall fall upon them the moment they walk in agreement.   It's so much peace when you abide as **One.** Your marriage will be argument-free when you're in **One** accord. Many don't believe this, however, there is a level of peace in God that you and your spouse never have to disagree, but thou must be perfectly joined together to accomplish this. Husbands and wives should be identical in their ways. Nothing has to differ about them. They must submit to doing everything by the Spirit. Either you are with God or against Him.   Thou art against God if thou disagree with His Word. Husbands and wives must touch and agree with God together in order for Him to walk with thee and bless thy marriage.

CAN TWO WALK TOGETHER EXCEPT THEY BE AGREED? (AMOS 3:3)

When two become **One** everything they have belongs to **One** another.   They become closer than close.   My Lord has made their flesh **One.** Your spouse is not only a part of you, he/she is you. **One** shouldn't be recognized without the other **One.** You are no longer two people dating or having a friendly relationship, but

35

you are **One. One** in body, walking in **One** accord, having **One** Love, **One** Faith, **One** Baptism, **One** Lord, and following after **One** Spirit. Your secrets, thoughts, faults, hurts, tears, body, possessions, pain, money, fruits, and your problems belongs to **One** another in Christ My Lord. You both share the same life. This is to say, "my car, my money, my house, my child, my problem," and the rest of that **"MY"** bull is put to death when two become **One**.

WHEREFORE THEY ARE NO LONGER TWAIN BUT ONE FLESH. WHAT THEREFORE GOD HATH JOINED TOGETHER LET NO MAN PUT ASUNDER. (MATTHEW 19:6)

When two become **One**, they are no longer independent or separate individuals. However, they are a single entity. **One** should never be able to see his or herself without the other **One**. **One** is powerful because **One** cannot be divided by anything, so regardless of how many people or things come against a marriage, as long as couples stand as **One** they shall be steadfast and immoveable. Therefore, it's very important for couples to become **One** because only a divided house cannot stand. **One** can't be divided by **One** or **One** million. No matter how much hell comes against two people who are **One** in Christ and living by faith they cannot be separated. No one can divide **One** into two when a man and his woman are perfectly joined together as **One** because **One** is ten times stronger when two are merged together. Lies, jealousy, hatred, rage, threats, family, friends, principalities, and powers, cannot come in between **One**. Zero can't touch it. Their enemies can't break them and hell can't separate them because **One** is impossible to cut asunder unless allowed. Therefore, let no man come in between thy union. When two people think alike they walk in agreement which makes their relationship stronger. Satan will try to destroy what My Lord has bonded together. Therefore, many things will come against it. For **One** will find out how strong **One** is when all hell tries to come in between it. When times get drastic **One** must help the other **One**. When **One** is weak the other can strengthen the other **One**. When **One** gets sad, **One** can make the other **One** smile. When **One** cries, **One** can wipe the other **One's** eyes. When **One** gets down, **One** can lift the other **One** up. **One** never stops loving **One** self. **One** never makes the other **One** jealous. They must bear **One** another's burdens. **One** must pray night and day. **One** knows that no weapon formed against it can prosper. They should be **One** in knowledge, knowing My Lord. They are **One** in faith moving mountains, and speaking those things that are not as though they were. **One** is more precious than any jewel. Therefore, they should value **One** another greatly. **One** is not whole without the other **One**. **One** doesn't have separate living quarters, separate lives, separate families, or separate issues because **One** is not separate from the other. They are in **One** another's business and they are each other's business. **One** should never get tired of the other **One**. Thoughts of loving **One** another should be the strongest thoughts on **One's** mind. **One** is always in **One's** imagination. **One** thought connects two souls that are **One** in Christ and that thought should be Love. **One** respects and honors **One** another. **One** never does their enemies will because if **One** gives in, then **One** can't live. Therefore, **One** doesn't bow but **One** suffers greatly when **One** is fake.

One is powerful. **One** never hates, abuses, curses, fights, provokes, burns, or betrays the other **One**. **One** is tight and **One** follows hard after Christ. **One** greatly desires the other **One**, and their passion for **One** another is mutual. When **One's** thoughts touch and agree there is **One** connection, and at that point **One** Love is in foreplay. When their bodies touch and agree there shall be **One** eruption, and at that point **One** Love is in full motion. Being **One** means that you can make strong passionate love to **One** another, and touch **One** another's soul daily, having **One** for breakfast, lunch, dinner, and a midnight snack. Eat and drink till **One** is filled. Love **One** another without ceasing, and spill great measures of love, joy, and peace in **One** another's life. **One** yearns to be with the other **One,** and everything **One** needs to know, **One** shall learn. Although you're **One,** My Lord is head over the Man, and Man is Head over his woman. The man must obey his Head; likewise, the woman must obey her head. Couples should love spending quality time together sowing into **One** another. For when you are **One** you are no longer a segment of each other's life, you share the same life in Christ. As **One** in Christ thy will live, move, and have thy being, being **One** in the Spirit of My Lord giving God the Glory due His name and there is no compromising **One!**

ONE LOVE

A marital relationship was the first kind of relationship that existed between Man and Woman. Adam and Eve weren't friends, lovers, business partners, etc. before marriage. They were married from the day God brought her to Adam. The very moment Adam laid eyes on Eve he had no doubt in his mind that she was his wife. His first words to her were you are bone of my bone, flesh of my flesh, and he called her his woman. He saw them as One of a Kind. This is how every man should look at his wife. He should feel one with her and she should feel one with him. It was one love between them from the very beginning meaning they gave the same kind of love to one another so the relationship didn't feel off balance. One didn't feel like they were giving more than the other because God created both the male and female in his own image and likeness, thus they both walked in righteousness and holiness before him in the Garden. They naturally knew how to love one another according to His will. They had no knowledge of evil; therefore, they didn't know how to offend one another. They weren't disrespectful, selfish, dishonest, abusive, deceitful etc. because they weren't made to be that way. Their hearts were pure. so they didn't think any evil. Sin was not in the world, so divorce would have never been an option for them, because they would have never thought to do anything that could cause them to make divorce an option. The only thing they could do was love and enjoy one another in the perfect bond of peace happily in the presence of a loving God. They didn't have any traps or snares to be concerned about until the Serpent saw the joy they were experiencing and became envious of their Holy Matrimony. Therefore, he lied to them and tempted them with the objective of taking the joy and peace they had with God away.

In the beginning when My Lord made man, he made them male and female, Adam & Eve, one body. They had the character of God, which sums up to be love. Please notice that every creature My Lord had made he commanded the earth and the waters to bring them forth and to reproduce itself after its own kind. However, when he made man, He didn't command the earth nor the waters to bring them forth because the elements of the world doesn't have the wisdom to create such a wonder in the image and likeness of God. Out of all the fowls of the air, the beast of the field, and the fishes in the sea, couldn't anything compare to Man. The making of them was a powerful work that only God could perform, he basically recreated small models of himself, and that's why he call his people his little ones. Those who walk in the image of God are little versions of Him known as children of the light.

God watered the face of the earth, and superbly fashioned a man from the dust of the ground. It's mysterious how the Almighty God sculptured the body of man from mud. Every bone, organ, cell, etc. were created from the combination of water and dust. For wisdom had brought forth an amazing wonder. When My Lord created Adam he scooped up a ball of mud and molded him from the dust of the earth, but when he made Eve, he never went back to the dirt: but rather he extracted Adam's rib and formed a woman from Man.

AND THE LORD GOD CAUSED A DEEP SLEEP TO FALL UPON ADAM, AND HE SLEPT: AND HE TOOK ONE OF HIS RIBS, AND CLOSED UP THE FLESH THEREOF; AND THE RIB, WHICH THE LORD HAD TAKEN FROM MAN MADE HE WOMAN, AND BROUGHT HER UNTO MAN AND ADAM SAID THIS IS NOW BONE OF MY BONE, FLESH OF MY FLESH SHE SHALL BE CALLED WOMAN BECAUSE SHE WAS TAKEN OUT OF MAN. (GENESIS 2:21-23)

The woman was made from one of the Man's Ribs. When a woman understands where she came from and the purpose of the rib, she'll have a better understanding of her role as a wife.

Taking one of Adams ribs was wisdom because ribs provide support and protection. They form a cage securing the heart and the lungs, thus, the most important thing that woman need to secure on a man is his heart. Ribs help to expand the chest cavity which enables you to breathe better; therefore, a woman that does what she was created to do, will supply her husband the support he needs which will allow him to inhale and exhale smoothly. The quality of his life will be much better with her. The woman was originally made pure, but since sin entered the world and corrupted mankind, now a woman must be redeemed and molded into that vessel of mercy by the Hand of God before a man's heart will be able to safely trust in her.

Wives, if you are doing things that are causing the heart of your husband not to trust you examine your ways because maybe you're not functioning the way God created you to. If your actions are causing him pain and making life difficult for him, you're a dislocated rib. Something in life has injured you and until you are healed of your wounds, you'll cause more problems for a man instead of being what God created you to be, which is a blessing to his soul. Husbands your wife is your rib. She is your body and as a Man you must protect and take care of your body at all cost knowing that if you're doing things that could lead to your ribs being fractured, bruised, or broken you're proving yourself to be irresponsible, negligent and less than a man by not inflicting pain upon yourself!

Ephesians 5:28-29 So ought men to love their wives as their own bodies. He that loveth his wife loveth himself. For no man ever yet hated his own flesh; but nourisheth and cherisheth it, even as the Lord the church:

ONE IN MIND

BE YE OF ALL ONE MIND, HAVING COMPASSION ONE OF ANOTHER, LOVE AS BRETHREN, BE PITIFUL, BE COURTEOUS. (1PETER 3: 8)

When you get married and become husbands and wives, your are no longer twain, but one flesh. Being one in flesh sets the foundation to become one in mind. Once husbands and wives have succeeded in having oneness of mind, at that time they've become perfectly joined together. They'll walk in unison and experience the harmony of a beautiful relationship. One in mind simply means they think **ALIKE** and if they think alike in the soundness of mind, they will have the abundance of peace because they will understand and agree on their roles in the relationship. Very seldom, if ever will they bump heads because why would you argue with someone you agree with? A man will know his position as being the head of the woman yet under the authority of Christ thus leading her as Christ leads him. Likewise, the wife will know where she stands as a woman in subjection to her husband in everything as long as he's been lead by Christ. Both of them will give God His glory due his name bringing forth the good fruits of life.

Being one in mind eliminates a lot of drama and confusion. Disputes will be few to none in the marriage of those who walk in the mind of Christ. Not that there won't be moments of disagreements, but whenever challenges do arise if you have the mind of Christ those challenges will be dealt with wisely. The warmth that permeates between two people that think alike is an unexplainable peace. It will be a harmonious indivisible companionship and their bond will be impervious. Their tune of love will be as a beautiful melody of heaven. The Lovemaking will be much stronger and better because the chemistry of oneness is explosive. You'll know what your spouse likes and doesn't like, what he or she will and won't stand for. You'll know where each other stand on the issues of life. You'll agree on how to conduct yourselves in different settings and situations, and the love and respect you have for each other will be paramount. When thou art one in mind, two will always touch and agree, bearing witness to everything the other does and speaks, and will stand by each other through clear and cloudy situations. They will be confident that their spouse is in it to win it with them. If you seek God's face, and if you're in touch with yourself, you'll be in tune with your spouse. You will be able to easily detect the lies of the enemy. You will know what your spouse is and isn't capable of doing, so no one will be able to just walk up and feed you anything about your spouse. When you are one in mind, you'll never have to ask certain questions because you'll already know the answers. You will know each other so well, that at times you will be able to say the next word that will come out of each other's mouth. Christ taught us the power of one when he prayed that the people of God be as one even as He and His Father are one. He knew being one makes you invincible. Nothing will be impossible for couples that are one in mind to do and nothing will be able to stop them from doing it. The things they will be able to get accomplished together would be phenomenal, because being one in mind ensures that everything they set out to do will be accomplished. That business they want to open, the city they want to take over, the home they want built, etc. Anything they can imagine can be manifested as long as they walk in oneness. The power of one is clearly seen in the book of Genesis when the whole earth was one speech. As one, the people built a city and a tower that reached the heavens.

AND THE LORD SAID, BEHOLD THE <u>PEOPLE IS ONE</u>, AND THEY HAVE ONE LANGUAGE; AND THIS THEY BEGIN TO DO: AND NOW NOTHING WILL BE RESTRAINED FROM THEM WHICH THEY HAVE IMAGINED TO DO. (GENESIS 11: 6)

Understand, this is why Satan is attacking your marriage so strongly. He does not want you to ever experience the power of being ONE, because once you become one, you will be unstoppable. If you were to start agreeing with another and believing in one another your marriage will become like a fortress. The enemy wants to break you, so he surely doesn't want you to become one in mind with one another. He does his best to cause confusion. If he can get you and your spouse to start speaking two different languages he will divide your marriage, because the very moment you stop understanding one another, the very moment your marriage will begin to break down. God gives us a demonstration of this, when he wanted to separate all the people that were in one mind he confounded their language.

LET US GO DOWN, AND THERE CONFOUND THEIR LANGUAGE, THAT THEY MAY NOT UNDERSTAND ONE ANOTHER'S SPEECH. SO THE LORD SCATTERED THEM ABROAD FROM THENCE UPON ALL THE FACE OF THE EARTH: AND THEY LEFT OFF TO BUILD THE CITY. (GENESIS 11: 7, 8)

When two people think differently from each other their relationship will be unstable thus having a see-saw experience. One minute their marriage will appear to be going up and the next minute it's going down and this will be a continuous experience between them until they get on the same page or divorce. When you're not in one mind with one another, you will be wasting too much time and energy trying to figure each other out and it becomes tiresome trying to understand the mood swings, decisions, and actions of someone else. You can only wonder how or why this person thinks the way they think? And how can they do what they do and say the things they say? For example, when a couple gets angry at each other, if they think differently, one of them might go pray, while the other one go to the club. One might get quiet, while the other goes into a rage. One might read the bible, while the other goes and have a secret love affair. One has taken the right step but when the other takes the wrong step, they're traveling in opposite directions, thus moving further apart. They'll eventually have to part ways or live in misery together. When two people don't think alike they will constantly dispute over any and everything regardless of how small or big the issue may be. They will not be able to secure each other's heart. Where as if they thought alike, they both would go pray, they both will know when to be quiet, they both will read the word and their relationship will become stronger in the end.

Too many married couples are living in discord. All they do is argue, fuss, and fight. They can't enjoy one another, primarily because they can't agree on anything. When couples don't understand one another it's as though they are speaking in tongues with no interpreter. It gets aggravating when you're trying to explain something to someone who cannot comprehend a word that you are saying to them. They'll take everything you say out of context. If they have a completely different definition for the words you speak although you may be saying the same things that their saying, they'll comprehend you to mean something totally different from what you're saying to them. Regardless of how many times you repeat yourself or how many different ways you try to explain it, they cannot get it. Couples who never reach a point of understanding can't get anything accomplished and usually end up separating, divorced, or remain unhappy together. Don't allow Satan to come in your home and confound your language. Always pray to understand one another that you may remain in one accord and accomplish everything that you bothy have set out in your mind to do.

HAVE COMPASSION ON ONE ANOTHER. For example, a woman gets into a car accident and incurs minor injuries, but the car was totaled. Her husband gets very upset with her because they only had liability on the car and the accident was her fault. As a man, he should be very thankful that she is okay and be sympathetic towards her for having to experience that incident. He need to be encouraging her by telling her, "Baby don't worry about the car because that can be replaced, the most important thing is that you are ok. Losing a car is nothing but losing you is everything, so let's worship God together and praise him for keeping you safe." However, A man that has no compassion resorts to calling his wife stupid, careless, irresponsible, etc. He makes her feel worse than how she already feels. It's obvious by his heartless remarks he prefer that the car was spared before she was. Couples that lack compassion for each other show that they can careless about each other. This should not be the case. Always be sympathetic towards one another.

LOVE AS BRETHREN husband and wives are brothers and sisters in the Lord and should love another accordingly. Understand men, that your woman is your wife on earth, but your sister in Christ, so don't only love her as your wife but love and treat her as though she is your sister. Likewise wives, understand that your man is your husband on earth, but he is your brother in Christ, so don't only love him as your husband but love and treat him as your brother. As brother and sister you suppose to look out for one another.

Throughout the course of your marriage unexpected situations are going to always arise in your marriages and some of them will be unfortunate events. During those events it will be very necessary for couples to *BE PITIFUL* towards one another. Pitiful means to tender-hearted, therefore, you should be soft hearted towards your spouse. Example, if a man suddenly loses his job, a woman shouldn't panic, get mad, or make him feel as though he's less of a man, but as his wife she should be soft-hearted and reassure him that she got his back and to trust that God shall provide for them and open up other greater doors for him. When couples are pitiful towards each other it medicates the wounds that life has afflicts on them. It's the healing touch your spouse need from you when they've been diagnosed with illnesses, experienced a tragedy, and or going through any trial of life.

Married couples need to prepare themselves for the unexpected situations by sitting down and expressing their sentiments on vital issues that has caused other marriages to fail. They need to discuss the best way to handle or prevent those issues from knocking at their door. If they were to come together beforehand and discuss those topics they could avoid falling into many of the same traps others have. Example, many men go to war with their wives over certain clothes that they don't feel is appropriate for her to wear in public. This issue alone has been the root of the arguments in many households. However, If couples were to discuss matters such as these before they arose and establish certain guidelines a problem shouldn't arise unless one deviate from the path of understanding. When you discuss common problems that occur in many marriages and come to an understanding beforehand it eliminates a high probability of those problems occurring in your marriage. When two people walk in agreement they will think alike having the same judgment and speaking the same things toward agreed upon issues that, if they were not of one mind could cause division between them.

Most successful businesses became successful not because of the product they were offering, but because of the customer service they provided. Understand there is nothing better than good customer service. A person don't mind paying more and will become a faithful customer of yours when their being treated right. They will highly recommend your services to others. On the contrary, it doesn't matter how good the product is, if you have poor customer service many will not support your establishment. If the staff is rude or snobbish it will run people away. This same principle applies in marriage. Your attitude towards your spouse is highly important for your marriage to last, so **BE COURTEOUS** to one another. No man or woman wants to come home to a moody spouse. It doesn't matter how hard you work, how much you provide, how good you clean, how many things you do, if you have a foul attitude he or she won't have any desire to be around you, therefore always be friendly to your spouse. Your attitude should be pleasant. If you're courteous to one another you will respect each other's feelings. When you're courteous to another you will open up doors for each other. You will check to be sure your spouse doesn't need for you to bring him or her anything before you get home. You will greet them at the door with a kiss. You will do all things for one another without murmuring or disputing with each other. You will be thoughtful and considerate of each other's feelings.

ONE IN PRAYER

AGAIN I SAY UNTO YOU THAT IF TWO OF YOU SHALL AGREE ON EARTH AS TOUCHING ANYTHING THAT THEY SHALL ASK, IT SHALL BE DONE FOR THEM OF MY FATHER WHICH IS IN HEAVEN FOR WHERE TWO OR THREE ARE GATHERED TOGETHER IN MY NAME THERE AM I IN THE MIDST OF THEM. (MATTHEW 18:19, 20)

One of the very most important and necessary things for married couples to do in order for them to STAY together is to be one in prayer. Prayer is powerful. It is communication with the Almighty God and under any circumstance you should always pray together. It should be a part of your everyday lifestyle. Prayer truly changes things and through prayer all of your dreams can come true. However, before praying together, make sure that you and your spouse are dwelling and walking together in unity because the promise is, where two are touching anything on earth in agreement, their request shall be granted. That promise is better than any genie, a wishing well, or luck charm can give you, being that unity in prayer not only yields unlimited power but is guaranteed to be fulfilled. Nothing will be withheld from couples that touch and agree in prayer. The moment they come together in his name they can experience the presence and power of Christ. He will be right there among them. This is why Satan works diligently to keep up commotion in marriages. He knows if he can cause wars in the house, your prayers won't be answered.

FROM WHENCE COME WARS AND FIGHTINGS AMONG YOU? COME THEY NOT HENCE, EVEN OF YOUR OWN LUST THAT WAR IN YOUR MEMBERS? YE LUST, AND HAVE NOT, YE KILL, AND DESIRE TO HAVE, AND CANNOT OBTAIN: YE FIGHT AND WAR, YET YE HAVE NOT BECAUSE YE ASK NOT. YE ASK NOT, AND _RECEIVE NOT,_ BECAUSE YE ASK AMISS, THAT YOU MAY CONSUME IT UPON YOUR LUSTS. (JAMES 4: 1-3)

Satan knows God is a God of peace and that you can't go to God with war and hatred in your heart for one another and expect for him to grant you your request. God honors the voice of them that obey Him, so as long as the devil have you two acting like fools, you hindering the blessings of God upon you. You can't be at war in the flesh and try to give glory to God in the Spirit. Thou can't tell each other to go to hell in one breath, and five seconds later scream "Halleluiah, thank you Jesus!" Thou can't verbally or physically abuse one another in one instance, then worship, praise, and lift up "unholy" hands to him in the next instance. If your house is full of war and confusion don't even think about giving God praise just quiet the noise.

BETTER IS A DRY MORSEL, AND QUIETNESS THEREWITH, THAN A HOUSE FULL OF SACRIFICES WITH STRIFE. (PROVERBS 17:1)

In the midst of an argument with your mate, don't start praising the name of the Lord in attempts to drown out their voice. It's evil of you to start screaming Halleluiah, Thank You Jesus as a means of tuning them out. Nor can you be at home acting a fool, disrespecting and cursing one another out then go to Church and give God the sacrifice of praise. It saddens God to witness those he joined together living in discord. He died that you may have an abundant life not for you two to live like vicious animals attacking one another. If you know your house isn't in order, be quiet until you get your house in order. Before you offer God a praise, a gift, a tithe, etc establish peace with another immediately. Before you fix your lips to praise him you need to fix the issues you have with your mate first. because the Lord is not going to co-sign on your madness.

THEREFORE IF THOU BRING THY GIFT TO THE ALTER, AND THERE REMEMBEREST THAT THY BROTHER HATH OUGHT

AGAINST THEE; LEAVE THERE THY GIFT BEFORE THE ALTAR, AND GO THY WAY; → FIRST ← BE RECONCILED TO THY BROTHER, AND THEN COME OFFER THY GIFT(Matthew 5: 23)

Until you restore peace in your house your prayers will be hindered; therefore, making peace with your spouse should be your first priority. Don't let things drag on for days unresolved. Don't hold grudges against one another because you will never be able to get those things you want for your marriage from God, until you dwell together in unity. Our God is Love, He gave us His Spirit that we may walk in his love, give his love and embrace his love and husbands and wives should have the greatest love for one another. His Holy Spirit empowers you to become a son of God, so it grieves his Spirit when you're acting like children of the devil. Repent quickly and understand that God won't lead your marriage nowhere until the waters are still in it. After couples have humbled themselves and turned from their wicked ways, then He will open his ears to your prayers. God hears the voice of those who dwell in one accord. His eyes behold all their ways and their house shall be a holy habitation. Blessed shall they be going in and blessed shall they be going out. If you and thou spouse are going through trying times, and all you two seem to do is strive against one another unceasingly, acknowledge that demonic spirits has set up camp in your house. You should immediately confess thy faults to one another, and forgive one another. Take some holy oil, which is pure olive oil and anoint each wall in the house in the name of Jesus. Rebuke all demons and command them to get out of thy house and ask God to cover your house with the Blood. Come together and pray.

Recite This Prayer

Dear Heavenly Father, thou art Righteous and Holy. Let your presence dwell amongst us. Lord, we request that you bring us into a closer fellowship with you. Teach me and my spouse how to love one another. Close every door in our life that is hindering us from coming closer together and open those doors that will bring us into a closer relationship with you. Multiply the fruits of our Spirit that you may be glorified in us and that we may have more love, joy, and peace to give to one another. Give us the mind and heart to do your will and have your way with us. As we yield ourselves to you, mold us to be a blessing and continue to bless, guide, and protect us. Forgive us of all our sins, and remove any bitterness and malice we might have in our hearts. Teach us to be patient with one another as we grow and learn from our mistakes. Let your Word dwell in us richly, and deliver us from all evil. Cover our house with the blood of Jesus and let your angels encamp around us. We know that you are able to do exceedingly and abundantly above all that we can ask or think. We stand in agreement on your Word and have faith that this marriage is built to last.

In Jesus Name, Amen

ONE IN KNOWLEDGE

LIKEWISE, YE HUSBANDS, DWELL WITH THEM ACCORDING TO KNOWLEDGE, GIVING HONOUR UNTO THE WIFE, AS UNTO THE WEAKER VESSEL, AS BEING HEIRS TOGETHER OF THE GRACE OF LIFE, THAT YOUR PRAYERS BE NOT HINDERED.(1 PETER 5:7)

If you want your marriage to last it is highly important to be doers of the Word of God and not hearers only, that the fruits of righteousness be manifested in your relationship. If you're not a DOER of his word you cannot bring forth love, joy, peace etc. This is why many church goers experience divorce because they went to Church and heard the Word, but went home and didn't do the Word, thus they deceived themselves. As a doer of the Word a man needs to feed his wife the Word of God daily. He should teach her the Way of God that they may dwell together as one in the knowledge of the Holy One. Their growth, strength, direction, and deliverance come through the revelation of Jesus Christ, so it's essential that couples water their marriage with the Word. They cannot take his Word for granted. All the knowledge, wisdom, and understanding that a man and woman have, they are commanded to share and dwell together according to it, that they be equally mature believers in Christ. They need to be on the same page when it come to knowing how to love, communicate, handle conflicts, and respect one another. They understand and respect each other's position and purpose of marriage according to the Word. They need to be on one accord regarding all things. Dwelling together according to knowledge ensure they will agree, respect and honor what comes out of each other's mouth. When couples are not on the same level of maturity in Christ it could cause many problems. One will be spiritually stronger than the other. One will find more delight in doing spiritual things, while the other could find more pleasure in worldly things. They will argue over simple issues such as going to Church. Example, the man may feel it's necessary for both of them to go Church where as his wife feel it's not necessary to go to Church in order to have a relationship with God. However, if they dwell together according to knowledge they both will agree that going to Church isn't necessary to have a relationship with God, but they'll also agree that going to church is the will of God because his Word says forsake not the assembling together of saints.

Issues often arise between many married couples when one feels that he or she has been in Christ longer than the other and becomes lifted with pride. For example, a woman that's been in church all her life may think it qualifies her to know more than her husband, who is a new convert, thus she won't listen to anything he has to tell her concerning the Word. The truth is the amount of time you've been attending Church has absolutely nothing to do with the measure of your knowledge and faith in God. God has the power to accelerate a man's growth by opening his eyes, and giving him quick understanding of His Word. For this reason, a woman who has been in the body of Christ longer than her man shouldn't think for one moment, that it qualifies her to be more spiritual,or that God can't quickly equip her husband with the wisdom he needs to effectively teach and lead her. For the steps of a good man are ordered by My Lord. Therefore, regardless to how much more spiritually mature a woman may think she is, if her husband's steps are ordered by My Lord, her show of maturity is seen when she humbles herself and follow her man. If she wars against that "good man", she's rebelling against the Word of God which expose that she's not spiritually mature at all. This does not imply that a woman can't be used by God to enlighten her man on some things. However, she must always know where she stands as a woman and not exalt herself against the knowledge of Jesus Christ. Nor should she condemn her husband or revoke his license to lead her whenever he does make mistakes, but be understanding that we all make mistakes and give him the space he needs to learn and grow from his mistakes.

Contrary to the way others think, she should always and at all costs follow him in spite of his shortcomings. She should never think just because she's been in Church longer than him that she knows more than him because many people that's been in Church their whole life still have no clue of who Christ is. In most cases, people who think like this haven't necessarily been active in Christ, however, they've been an active member of the local Church for a lengthy period of time, and being in the Church for years doesn't mean you know a thing about God. Lack of maturity causes one to think that anyone who hasn't been in Church as long as he or she has (or if you don't meet certain specifications of men), you can't be a vessel chosen by God to teach or feed them anything. Let this point be made again, being an active member of the local Church and being a follower of Christ is completely different. Don't be a hearer of the Word only, deceiving your own selves, but be a doer of the Word because it's the doers of the Word that are just before God. You should not forsake the assembly of saints meaning you should go to Church and fellowship with the people of God, however, it's more important that you walk worthy of the Lord of Glory. Those that attend Church, but never repent and bear their cross are usually the first ones to scream that they're saved, sanctified, and Holy Ghost filled, but those devils are a lie.

It's important for a man to pray and study to show himself approved of God and as he gains understanding of the Word of God, he will be able to strengthen and lead his woman accordingly. His wife is the weaker vessel in need of his strength, support, and of his loyalty to God. As My Lord pours into him, he in turn, must water the seed that is in his woman's heart that they may grow together. Couples need to be attentive to each other's wants and needs. They should be each other's greatest investments by sow deeds of love into another, blessing one another and walking in One Accord.

CHAPTER THREE

DIVINE ORDER

3

DIVINE ORDER

BUT I WOULD HAVE YOU TO KNOW THAT AT THE HEAD OF EVERY MAN IS CHRIST; AND THE HEAD OF THE WOMAN IS THE MAN; AND THE HEAD OF CHRIST IS GOD. (1Corinthians. 11:3)

Since the beginning, God had structure for everything. He created Adam and Eve to rule, but when Adam stepped out of order and disobeyed his Voice, everything fell out of order. Sin took position where man should have had control. However, when Christ manifested and died for our iniquities, He destroyed the power of sin and death, redeemed us from the enemy's hand, and took dominance over man. Men no longer have to be driven by evil desires and lusts, but can be led by the wisdom of God once they believe and submit to the Lordship of Christ.

In Christ, marriage is given a divine order. The chain of command goes as follows; God is head of Christ, Christ is head of every man, and man is head of woman. As a man holds on to Christ, the woman should hold on to her man. Whenever a man needs guidance, strength, and help, all he has to do is pray and obey his head, and a woman is commanded to assist and follow her husband. She should always acknowledge that he is her head, her king, and her lord for King David once spoke.

THE LORD SAID UNTO MY LORD SIT THOU AT MY RIGHT HAND, TILL I MAKE THINE ENEMIES THY FOOTSTOOL? (MATTHEW 22:44)

As King David said "The Lord" referring to God and then spoke saying "My Lord" meaning Christ. Husbands and wives can do the same. A man of God can say, "The Lord (referring to God the Father) said unto My Lord," My Lord meaning Christ. Likewise, the wife can say, "The Lord said unto My Lord..." However, she will be referring to "The Lord" (meaning Christ) said unto "My Lord" means her husband. It does not offend

Christ for a woman to call her husband lord, because her husband is her lord, and Jesus is the Lord of Lords. We are royalty in the Kingdom of God. Some women will never refer to their husband as their lord because they believe in doing so, that it would be making him equivalent to God, and that is not true. Calling thy husband lord is not only a show of honor to his God-given position as the head, but she also is declaring her position as being his queen.

AS SARA OBEYED ABRAHAM <u>CALLING HIM LORD</u> WHOSE DAUGHTER YE ARE IF YOU DO WELL. (1PETER 3:6)

The Gospel teaches that Sarah was a holy woman of My Lord who referred to her man as lord; this is why women like Sarah are altogether. Sarah she gave Abraham great respect through her obedience to him and showed her humility by calling him lord. Although she was a very physically attractive and many men lusted after her beauty, but she understood that true beauty is so much more than skin deep and walked accordingly. She beautified herself with a meek and quiet spirit meaning she submitted to Abraham. She was a wise woman that trusted in God.

1 Peter 3:3-5 Whose adorning let it not be that outward adorning of plaiting the hair, and of wearing of gold, or of putting on of apparel; But let it be the hidden man of the heart, in that which is not corruptible, even the ornament of a meek and quiet spirit, which is in the sight of God of great price. For after this manner in the old time the holy women also, who →trusted in God, adorned themselves, being →in subjection unto their own husbands:

If Sarah arrayed in all her beauty was humble enough to call her husband lord, why do many women of today think it's inappropriate to do so? Pride prevents them from doing such things and God hates pride. When a woman is walking worthy her inner beauty will be what her husband adores most about her and she will be considered to be one of the blessed daughters of Sarah. Therefore, a godly woman shouldn't mind applying the ways of Sarah in their life seeing that her ways were the ways of God. Many people will argue claiming that times have changed, which is somewhat true, and though the world may change, the Word never changes. The same sins that were committed then are being committed now, and the same Word that delivered man from sin back then, is the same Word that delivers us now. Therefore, be not conformed to this world, but be ye transformed by the renewing of your mind. The Love of God and His holiness will never change, but grows stronger. Though the world may be forever changing, we are commanded to be unlike those that are given to change. We should be steadfast and immoveable. Don't lose your integrity for anything or anybody. As children of God we are a powerful people able to do things by the Spirit of God that unbelievers can't do or understand, because they're not of the Spirit. However, those led by the Spirit will love their spouse differently from those who are in their flesh. The flesh wars against the Spirit; therefore, family, friends, coworkers, and all others that are in their flesh should speak against your marriage. If they're not hating on and coming against your marriage, examine yourself and make sure you're walking after the Spirit. Flesh should never be in agreement with thee. The way you love, honor, and respect one another should cause all those that doeth evil to hate the light. They should be persecuting you.

Many men compromise their position as head of the house in order to please their wives. They let their wives have their way, thus, hardening their hearts at the voice of My Lord. When they step out of the will of My Lord in order to please their wife, the cares of the world enters their heart and choke the seed, which in turns hinders the good fruits of righteousness from developing in the marriage because their doing things the wrong way. Regardless of how another way of doing things might appear to be right, My Lord hates every false way, and anytime things are not done His way, then it's the wrong route to take. Every avenue outside of Jesus Christ is unfruitful. Couples must stop bringing in their own concepts and philosophies on how they think the house should be kept. For there is no foundation outside of the Word of God that is built to last; therefore, stop doing things contrary of the Word of God because it won't work. Some things bring a false sense of peace and security, but it will eventually crumble. Jesus is the only way!

When men refuse to humble themselves and submit to the Gospel of Jesus Christ they are about to experience a great fall.   A man cannot keep or put his house in order unless he follows orders.   Far too many men are trying to bring their wives under subjection, but they're going about it the wrong way, and a man shouldn't expect for My Lord to deal with his wife until after he has handled him first. Adam was formed first, then Eve. Therefore, expect God to perfect those things concerning the man before He deal with the woman.   Christ is the boss of the house and if you are a good man your steps will be ordered in his Word. He'll direct your path concerning which church to attend, which city to live in, how to raise your children, etc.   There shouldn't be any compromising of fifty-fifty or seventy five-twenty five. Husbands and wives can't take turns being in control. Each should give one hundred percent in fulfilling their position.   Christ is head of man, and man is head of woman and that's all to it. You can't add or take from it. Christ being head of man leads the man and man being head of woman leads the woman.

FOR THE HUSBAND IS THE HEAD OF THE WIFE, EVEN AS CHRIST IS THE HEAD OF THE CHURCH: AND HE IS THE SAVIOUR OF THE BODY. THEREFORE AS THE CHURCH IS SUBJECT UNTO CHRIST, SO LET THE WIVES BE TO THEIR OWN HUSBANDS <u>IN EVERY THING</u>. (EPHESIANS 5:23, 24)

Everything means everything; that leaves nothing out. A woman should do whatever her husband says. As long as she knows he's a man of God then she knows he's a man led by Christ and her obedience to her husband is a reflection of her trust in My Lord. She knows in following her husband that she's following Christ and as long as her husband follows Christ, God is in control. However, some men make it difficult for a woman to trust and obey them because they are not humbling themselves under the mighty hand of God. They're doing things that are obviously out of the will of God and trying to convince their woman to follow them but it's understandable when a woman refuse to follow their husbands whenever they don't hear God's voice in them. If a man is trying to lead his woman into sinful things she should not follow him but pray, continue to be good and love her husband, and wait on God.

The man is the glory of God, but if My Lord can't get glory from a man, that man shouldn't expect to get glory from his woman. He needs to examine his ways and follow the divine order because how can any man expect for My Lord to put his house in order when he is out of order. In conclusion, in order for marriage to be established upon the rock husband and wives must follow the Divine Order.

DECLARATION OF LOVE

Esther 1:20 And when the king's decree which he shall make shall be published throughout all his empire, (for it is great,) all the wives shall give to their husbands HONOUR, both to great and small.

DEFINTION OF HONOUR
Original: *יקר*
Transliteration: *yeqar*
Phonetic: *yek-awr'**
BDB Definition*:# price, value, preciousness, honour, splendour, pomp## preciousness## price## honour, esteem

Marriage is a declaration of love. The day you said "I DO" you declared to the World that you loved that man or that woman and in declaring your LOVE for them, you are saying so many things in one word. One of those things is that you honour thy spouse. Many people don't understand or know the importance of honour. Honour means: to esteem, a person you hold in higher regard or superior standing, privileged, preciousness, value, and distinguished from others. Those who you honour aren't treated like a common thing or someone meaningless to you. They are sanctified in your life, and they are shown by the amount of honour that you bestow upon them, just how much they are worth to you. Husband and wives are supposed to give one another the highest honour and in giving thy spouse that honour, you're showing him or her that they are more precious to you than anything else in your life. You're also showing your spouse that only he or she has certain rights and benefits with you that others don't have. They are the only ones that can touch you intimately. They are the only ones that can whisper pillow talk in your ear. You will give them more respect than others. Example, when you honour your spouse the most, you may not answer the phone every time people call you, but every time your spouse calls, you'll be sure to answer his or hers ASAP. Everyone can't interrupt whatever it is your doing and get your assistance, but your spouse can. Nobody else can ask or tell you certain things, but your spouse can. You will always acknowledge them and whenever he or she speaks; your ears are open to them, having the highest regard for their opinions and feelings. It's very important for husbands and wives to honour one another in order to maintain a healthy and fruitful marriage. When you honour your spouse, your showing the world that they are distinguished among others, because only her or him are privileged to have it like THAT with you, and your enemies will be envious of the fact that only your spouse GOT IT LIKE THAT!

Husbands and wives the day you married one another, you gave each other the highest position of honour that anyone can hold in your life under God. So respect the position you gave them the privilege of having at all times. You should conduct yourself in a manner that honours them, even when they're not in your presence. When your enemies observe the Honour you give one another they will be envious of your relationship. All of your ex's and those that desire you are going to be jealous, because of the fact that they don't have it like that with you. Be sure to resist the devil when he tempts you to dishonor one another, knowing only Satan will influence you to do such a thing. The more you honour your spouse the more you strengthen your marriage. Honour is a key ingredient to the vitality of your marriage, as it is in everything you value. People that value their position in their secular job will keep their companies policies and honour their supervisor. Likewise, if you care about your marriage; you will honour your spouse and foremost importantly if you care about your relationship with God, you will honour His Word and HONOUR ONE ANOTHER.

HONOUR THY HUSBAND

Esther 1:12 But the queen Vashti refused to come at the king's commandment by his chamberlains: therefore was the king very wroth, and his anger burned in him.

In the Book of Esther, one of the greatest nuggets of wisdom concerning marriage given to us is the importance of a woman honoring her husband. Wives you might not agree with your husband on everything and sometimes you may not like his disposition but bear your cross, trust in the Lord, and submit to him. Many households are full of strife and marriages are ending in divorce, because of the woman not honoring her man. The man has been appointed head of his woman, so wives don't behave as though he can't "TELL" you what to do. If he tells you to come, then come. If that man wants you to go with him somewhere "GO". If he tells you to change your outfit, then change your attire. As long as he's not asking you to do anything foolish or that goes against God, then honour that man. Many women especially those with an independent woman's mindset, will have a problem with honoring their man, because their belief is that no man can tell them what to do. They feel that by submitting to their husband, their giving him control and that's something that an independent woman refuses to do. One of the common remarks they'll throw in their husband's face is, "You don't tell me what to do, you're not my father." and they are correct in one thing; their husband is not their father. However, God has given the husband authority over his wife, so he should be given higher honour than her father so his words should be highly respected. Wives never compare your husband to your father. Number one, they are in two separate categories and secondly a man doesn't marry you to raise you into a woman. Hopefully, He married you because he loves every bit of the woman that your father helped groomed you to become and as his wife you'll honour him as your husband. When you're married you cannot bring an independent woman's mindset into your marriage and expect a healthy marriage.

WIVES SUBMIT YOURSELVES UNTO YOUR OWN HUSBANDS, AS UNTO THE LORD. (EPHESIANS 5:22)

Wives if you honour your husband as you should, you would submit to him AS unto the Lord. Others may accuse you of always letting him have his way but that's not letting him have his way. That's you doing thing's God's way and through obedience to his commandments; you are operating in the ways of peace. This is the same reason why many women don't have peace in their marriage, because they will not honour their husband and some of those same women will call to mock you, by saying foolish things such as: " Girl every time he tells you to jump, you say How high." Don't allow them haters to influence you from obeying the Word of God, but continue to honour your husbands, as unto the Lord. This is by no means saying that your husband is the Lord, but by honoring him AS unto the Lord, you're showing everyone that Christ is your Lord.

On the seventh day, when the heart of the king was merry with wine, he commanded Mehuman, Biztha, Harbona, Bigtha, and Abagtha, Zethar, and Carcas, the seven chamberlains that served in the presence of Ahasuerus the king, to bring Vashti the queen before the king with the crown royal, to shew the people and the princes her beauty: for she was fair to look on. But the queen Vashti refused to come at the king's commandment by his chamberlains: therefore was the king very wroth, and his anger burned in him. (Esther1:10-12)

In the book of Esther, King A-has-u-e'rus had just finished showing the glory of his Kingdom. He was having a seven-day feast for all of the people present in the Palace both small and great. At the same time, his wife had her own activity going on, by having a feast for all of the women in the Royal House. The King had sent for his wife to come to him, so that he may show off her beauty. This is a common thing that many men like to do, because men love to hear other men talk about how beautiful of a woman he has. However, the king's fascination over her beauty may have given her a false sense of security, because she somehow thought that she could dishonor her man without suffering any consequences from it. But there is a cause & effect to every decision that we make in life. The king learned that beauty is vain, because regardless of how intoxicated he was from her beauty, he sobered up quickly the moment she dishonored him. Understand wives, it takes much more than beautifying your body to a make a man happy, learn from Queen Vashti's experience, because her beauty was enough to get the Kings attention and even enough to get him to marry her, but it wasn't enough to keep him with her. A man can be head over heels with how beautiful you are and may love driving you all around the world showing you off like you're a brand new car, but if you don't honour him, his perception of you could change immediately. He'll go from looking at you like you were a brand New Bentley, to looking at you like you're a broken down hoopty and his desires for you will fade away. Many men don't desire to touch their wives sexually because their wives are not respecting them and because of that lack of respect, it won't matter how good you look to everybody else, you won't look good to him. The honour you give to that man is what brings him glory. Queen Vashti's beauty made no difference to the King "after" she dishonored him because "Honour" is more important to a "Man", than how beautiful she is to him. A lot of women wonder why their homes fell apart or why their man has lost physical desires for them, especially those women who are beautiful enough that many men are running through their door lusting them, but it requires much more than being physically attractive to a "man" to keep a man. If you have an arrogant attitude, a sassy mouth, a stubborn spirit, etc, although the world may be applauding you for your "looks", he's more concerned about how you're making him look. So when you dishonor him, you're not making him look good at all. Again, this is why the fire has burnt out in many marriages. So if you're wondering why your husband doesn't jump your bones like he use to, it could very well be that you're not honoring him, so he doesn't desire you the way he use to. Wives never put confidence in your physical appearance because your outward beauty is not the deciding factor in determining whether or not your marriage will be fruitful and lasting. Beauty is vain; understand that it's the honour you give to your man that determines how beautiful you are in his eyes. Any woman that lifts herself up thinking she's too independent, too fine, and/or too successful to submit to her man is full of pride and arrogance. She may have what some men want but she is not anything that a man needs. The woman was created for the man, so if men didn't exist what would be the woman's purpose? God designed her to be a man's help meet so without the man, the woman has no divine purpose. Yet the beauty of their skin has caused some of them to become arrogant and prideful which has corrupted their heart, thus they've become of no good use to a man. Pride and arrogance are two of the seven abominations that My Lord hates and many marriages have ended because of a woman's arrogance and pride. Wives if your heart has been contaminated with these two great evils, pray God purifies your hearts by faith, because only the pure in heart shall see God.

Also wives, if you're not respecting that man as your husband, what is stopping you from having an affair on him? A woman that doesn't honour her husband has much greater potential to step outside of her husband, than one that does. Her show of dishonor reveals to others that she doesn't care about her husband, and that causes others not to honour her as a married woman, and they will disrespect her husband since she doesn't value him. Nothing good can come to a woman that dishonors her man. Evil news reports will he spread on her.

FOR THIS DEED OF THE QUEEN SHALL COME ABROAD TO ALL WOMEN, SO THAT THEY SHALL DESPISE THEIR HUSBANDS IN THEIR EYES, WHEN IT SHALL BE REPORTED THE KING A-HAS-U-E'RUS COMMANDED VASHTI THE QUEEN TO BE BROUGHT IN BEFORE HIM, BUT SHE CAME NOT. (ESTHER 1:17)

Wives if you're not honoring your husband you stand a great chance of losing your husband. Understand that a man cannot be happy with you if you do not honour him, so wives think before you act. It only leads to shame and disgrace. Some women were like queen Vashti, they were with men who gave them the utmost respect, but due to their acts of dishonor they lost a good man. For example, the life of Vashti drastically changed because of one poor decision. She went from being highly exalted and treated like royalty, to being an outcast and clothed with shame. Her rebellion changed her entire future. Likewise, with many women of today they went from being one man's wife (queen) to being treated like another man's trash. They digressed from a position of honour to shame, solely because they refused to honour a man. Vashti's blessing was given to another woman that walked worthy of it. As the old saying goes, "what one person won't do, another will" and this is why some men are having an affair on their wives. Every time his woman won't come to him when he call for her, every time she won't bring him his plate, every time she won't make love to him, encourage, support, talk sweet to him, go places with him, respond diligently to his needs, she is pushing him away from her, right into the arms of other women waiting in line to happily serve him. Therefore wives, give your man no reason to seek the honour you should be giving him, in other places. No, it's not right for a man to do that, but many men are roaming the streets, going to clubs and having affairs and/or filing for divorce because that respect and honour is not at home. The truth is, if you're husband isn't worth fighting for, if you can't respect him as a man, if he can't tell you anything, if he's not being led by God, why did you marry him? Because as his wife your love should be so good to him, that he should feel like the biggest fool if he were to step outside of you or walk away from you, but that can only be possible if you honour him. In the case of the King he put away Vashti and found himself another queen that was not only beautiful in appearance, but beautiful in spirit and her name was Esther. She was all together lovely being beautiful inside and out and this is what every wife should be. She made it her business to please her him, and he loved every inch of her. This is another powerful lesson that God teaches us in this book of Esther concerning honour, which is a woman that honours her husband, is a better woman than the woman that doesn't honour her man. Her way of loving her man made her far more attractive in the eyes of men. She increases her husband's desire for her because she makes pleasing him her number one priority. Thus, she's not only fulfilling her divine purpose, but her man won't have any qualms with her, seeing that she never refuses him. Her ways provoke him to want to do anything for her and why wouldn't he, seeing that she will do anything for him. Wives learn from Queen Vashti's mistake, by being dishonorable to her husband, she forfeited her blessing to another woman that was more than willing to go all out for him. So if you want your marriage to last, don't repeat her mistakes but adopt the mindset of Ester and honour that man.

If it please the king, let there go a royal commandment from him, and let it be written among the laws of the Persians and the Medes, that it be not altered, That Vashti come no more before king Ahasuerus; and let the king give her royal estate unto another that is better than she. (Esther 1:19)

In conclusion, wives before you accuse your man of being possessive, make sure it's not you who is being disrespectful. As Queen Vashti, many of today's women would have accused the king of being petty, controlling, selfish, and inconsiderate. They'll call him petty and controlling because he not solely got angry with her for not coming to him, thus in their eyes, he made a big deal out of nothing. They'll call him selfish and inconsiderate because she was holding a feast with her female friends at the time he summoned her and since the only thing he wanted was to show off her beauty, he could've been more considerate of what she was doing. However, there are two sides to every story because in the eyes of men things are seen differently. Now Watch Closely.

1. What may be considered petty in a woman's eyes may be big in man's eyes as it is in this case. It was the PRINCIPLE of the matter that was GREAT. No husband should have to fight his wife to get the honour he deserves as her husband. Wives you may not like everything he requests of you or you may not like the time in which he requests it, but you shouldn't just say NO to him nor have that NOT NOW attitude with him without a good cause, because every time you refuse him, it could kindle strife between you two. It may seem as though he's tripping over nothing but No man wants to feel inferior, unimportant, or dishonored by his woman. Too many women falsely accuse their husbands of being "controlling" when the truth is, they're not honoring him. If a man is angry with you for not giving him the honour he deserves as your husband, that doesn't mean he's possessive or controlling. Do you call your "boss" controlling when he tells you to do something you dislike? Or is it you being insubordinate whenever you refuse to do something he tells you to do? Insubordination is grounds for termination without unemployment benefits; so if you value your position in your company you're going to honour your immediate supervisors. Likewise, as in the household, your husband is your immediate supervisor and if you value your

position in his life, then you need to respect that man because if you don't honour that man you're only pushing him away from you.

2. The Queen revealed that she was a Hypocrite, because had she not been married to the King and the King had summoned her, she would have immediately dropped everything she was doing and ran to the Kings Throne, but she thought since the King was her husband, she could get away with dishonoring him. So the lesson being taught here is this, whether he was a King or a peasant, she should have honored him because he was her Husband. Too many women are quick to honour their pastor, their doctor, their lawyer, their favorite celebrity, etc. because of those people's position in the world, but they won't honour their own husbands, who are supposed to have the highest position in their life. Women who have bestowed more honour upon other men provoke their men to jealousy. This is the reason some men don't even go to church because their wives glorify the Pastor. If you're the type of woman that receives the word from your pastor with no questions asked, but every time your husband tries to teach you the Word and you challenge him on everything he speaks, you're provoking him to jealousy. If you jump quickly whenever the pastor needs for you to do something, but your husband got to pull your teeth just to get you to do anything he needs, then you're provoking him to jealousy. He doesn't know if you're going to hear the Word or see the Pastor. You should honour the pastor as the minister of God, but he should never be given more honour than your husband, because whenever a man sees that another man has more control over his wife than he does, you're provoking him to jealousy and he can't be secure with you.

3. Wives, every time you dishonor your man you're challenging who he is as your husband, thus, you're making his position as head of the house harder for him. Just as some supervisors hate going to work and finding out that some have resigned from their position not because they hated the position itself, but because they hated dealing with some of their insubordinate coworkers, the same is true that some men hate coming home to their wife, and some have gotten a divorce because they couldn't find

happiness with a woman that didn't honour them. A man is supposed to guide his woman as the Lord guides him. He's supposed to teach her as the Spirit teaches him. He's supposed to make love to her unceasingly, but that's something he cannot perform, if he's married to a woman that won't honour him. When a woman gets to the point where she "refuses" to give her husband that respect due him, then she can't expect for the relationship to last. Any woman that has or develops an "independent woman's mindset" can expect to be without a man. Bottom line, if you want to keep the fire in your marriage burning brightly, Honour Thy Man.

Esther 1:20 And when the king's decree which he shall make shall be published throughout all his empire, (for it is great,) all the wives shall give to their husbands HONOUR, both to great and small.

WHEN NOT TO OBEY

1 Samuel 25:3, 33-34 Now the name of the man was Nabal; and the name of his wife Abigail: and she was a woman of good understanding, and of a beautiful countenance: but the man was churlish and evil in his doings; and he was of the house of Caleb.

Some husbands like to brow beat their wives with scriptures demanding obedience from them and although a woman is instructed to be obedient to her husband she is not required to be a fool for her husband. The only one we are required to be a fool for is Christ; therefore, in some situations it is very wise for a woman not to obey her husband. The perfect example of when it's good for a woman to counter act her husband is displayed between Nabal and Abigail. Abigail was a beautiful and wise woman that somehow was married to a fool. Her husband being an evil man had rendered evil to David who had been good to him. Nabal basically in so many words told David to "go to hell" after David requested food for protecting his possessions freely all day and night. Since Nabal chose to curse David instead of bless him, David had purposed in his heart to kill everything that had life in it that belonged to Nabal. After Abigail heard about her husband wrongful actions, she took it upon herself to rectify the situation.

But one of the young men told Abigail, Nabal's wife, saying, Behold, David sent messengers out of the wilderness to salute our master; and he railed on them ... Now therefore know and consider what thou wilt do; for evil is determined against our master, and against his entire household: for he is such a son of Belial that a man cannot speak to him. Then Abigail made haste, and took two hundred loaves, and two bottles of wine, and five sheep ready dressed, and five measures of parched corn, and an hundred clusters of raisins, and two hundred cakes of figs, and laid them on asses. (1 Samuel 25:14-18)

The actions of Abigail disheartened her husband, but it prevented evil from coming upon her household, because of her many lives were spared. Sometimes Ladies you may have to step aside of your man and do what's right in the eyes of God in order to save yourself, children, and many from danger. God is an understanding God and he surely doesn't want you to support your man when he is "obviously" wrong. If you see your husband mistreating people, talking to people any kind of way, etc. You don't know what someone has purposed in their heart to do; therefore, if it's in your power to rectify his wrongdoing, it would be very wise of you to do so. You may be very well saving yourself and others from wrath that your man has brought upon you all.

But it came to pass in the morning, when the wine was gone out of Nabal, and his wife had told him these things, that his heart died within him, and he became as a stone. And it came to pass about ten days after, that the LORD smote Nabal that he died. And when David heard that Nabal was dead, he said, Blessed be the LORD that hath pleaded the cause of my reproach from the hand of Nabal, and hath kept his servant from evil: for the LORD hath returned the wickedness of Nabal upon his own head. And David sent and communed with Abigail, to take her to him to wife. (1 Samuel 25:37-39)

Wives, learn from Abigail. She didn't tell her husband what she had done until "after" she did it. Had she told him her plans he would have prevented her from doing it, so as we see clearly her wisdom rewarded her in the end. God delivered her from her evil husband and put her in the arms of a Good Man!

Wives, if your man is ignorant or if he has decided to do something foolish, don't follow him down that destructive path because God will execute the same punishment upon you that he does upon your husband. God wants you to obey your husband, but if your husband leads you in a direction that's contrary to the word of God, then don't obey your husband. If you agree with him to do sinful things, you will suffer the same consequences as he. The word below shows a perfect example of a woman being destroyed because she agreed with her husband to tempt God!

AND PETER ANSWERED UNTO HER, TELL ME WHETHER YE SOLD THE LAND FOR SO MUCH? AND SHE SAID, YEA, FOR SO MUCH. THEN PETER SAID UNTO HER HOW IS IT THAT YE HAVE AGREED TOGETHER TO TEMPT THE SPIRIT OF THE LORD, BEHOLD, THE FEET OF THEM WHICH BURIED THY HUSBAND ARE AT THE DOOR, AND SHALL CARRY THEE OUT. THEN FELL SHE DOWN STRAIGHT WAY YEILDING UP THE GHOST: AND THE YOUNG MEN CAME IN, AND FOUND HER DEAD, AND CARRYING HER FORTH, BURIED BY HER HUSBAND. (ACTS 5: 8-10)

Again, let me re-emphasize that although the Word teaches that a woman should obey her husband in everything, it was written to women who are supposedly married to men led by God. However, whenever a woman acknowledges that she is married to a foolish man or that her husband is about to a make a wrong turn (foolish mistake), it's important that she does not follow him. Whenever he's about to do something dumb and ridiculous she must not agree with him and let him be on his own. It is **dangerous** for her soul when a woman follow her husband down the wrong path.   For example, in the above passage, Sapphira was married to a foolish man named Ananias and she had secretly agreed with him to withhold part of the money back from some of the land that God had commanded them to sell and to bring the purchase price to Him. Ananias entered in first and was slain by God for withholding the money and his wife entered in three hours later, not knowing what happened to her husband and was questioned rather or not her husband gave up the correct amount and she lied also. Note, all she had to do was **speak the truth**, but since she decided to lie along with her husband she fell dead also.   Never follow any voice that is leading you to sin regardless of who that person may be. Rather it's your husband, pastor, parents, boss, lawyer, etc. When your husband chooses not to obey the Word of God, let him do his own thing, but you sure to continue to obey the word of God. Anytime a man is trying to influence his wife to do any kind of deceitful or evil work she should not hearken to his voice. Men who try to lead their women into swinging, drugs, robbery, etc. are leading them both into the path of death. So many women are incarcerated, suffering, and dead because they chose to follow a foolish man. They conspired with their husband to steal, kill, and destroy the life and/or lives of others. They sold drugs with him, they lied for him, they allowed themselves to be the bait to set up others for robbery or murder, they agreed together to tempt the Lord. As with Sapphira, it didn't matter that she was a woman, she suffered the same consequences that her husband suffered. She chose her husband above the commandments of God. This is a perfect example of a woman who loved her man more than she loved God. Any woman that is following a man that's influencing her to go against the ways of God is in jeopardy of losing her soul unless she repents.

It's important for saints not to be unequally yoked together with unbelievers, so that you may avoid problems such as this. A person can't strengthen and encourage your walk in Christ if he/she doesn't believe in Christ. Example , a believer know that it's wrong to do deceitful work like cheating on their taxes, but someone who don't believe in the Word don't see any wrong in it and will influence you to do it for the financial rewards of it. However, the penalty for the sin is much greater than the money you may obtain or save from that deceitful work. God hates deceitful work: therefore, wives whenever your husband is trying to get you to rebel against the commandments of God do not hearken to his foolishness. Let that man be a fool by himself. Learn from Sapphire mistake and never agree with your husband to do anything that goes against God!

HONOUR THY WIFE

LIKEWISE, YE HUSBANDS, DWELL WITH THEM ACCORDING TO KNOWLEDGE, <u>GIVING HONOUR UNTO THE WIFE</u>, AS UNTO THE WEAKER VESSEL, AND AS BE HEIRS TOGETHER OF THE GRACE OF LIFE; THAT YOUR PRAYERS BE NOT HINDERED. (1PETER 3:7)

Though a man is the head of the house he is required to honour his wife as unto the weaker vessel, meaning number one, he can't abuse his authority over her. He must acknowledge that women were not created to be as physically strong as men, so their incapable of handling certain things that men can. As a man, don't you dare put burdens on her that you yourself won't bear, because a real man won't burden his wife with heavy loads even if she would carry them, knowing she is a weaker vessel. Yet many men do place heavy burdens on their spouses while they sit back playing video games night and day. They watch their wives carry 95% of the responsibility of the household while they only carry 5%. She didn't sign up(marry you) for that foolishness, she didn't marry you to baby sit you nor should your marriage be comparable to a slave and master relationship but a humble servant to a Loving Lord. Your wife is thy help mate, she is not your indentured servant, so neither talk nor treat her as such. Many wives work an eight-plus hour a day job just as their husbands. However, some men still expect for their wife to come home after work and cook, clean, look after the kids, iron his work clothes, wash and fold the laundry, walk the dogs, take out the trash, manage the bills, etc. without lifting a finger to help her. Meanwhile, while their wife is working like a Hebrew slave, he's goofing off, playing or watching sports, playing video games, on the computer, etc. What's even worse, he might be out with his friends, flirting and/or entertaining other women, speaking sweet things in their ear, being quick to spend his chump change on them in hopes of ravishing their bodies, and yet he won't spend a dime on his wife who's at home working like a slave keeping the house together. Then to top it off, he has the nerve to come home with an attitude and raise hell with his wife if the kitchen isn't clean. Men that do such things are Hypocrites of the worse kind. They are quick to try to massage every other woman's body, but if

77

their wife complains of a back ache, they won't even so much as offer her a backrub. Many so called ministers of God are guilty of this sort of hypocrisy because they're quick to attend to everybody else's needs at the church and run to their rescue, but they are irresponsive to their wives' needs. They use the excuse that God's will comes first, but if God's will came first, they would honour their spouse and take care of home first. Men don't claim to be "having mercy" on everybody else but meanwhile you're having no mercy on your wife. Don't turn the pastor's office into your play boy penthouse and have affairs with the women in your flock, but won't touch your wife at all when you get home. Men that do these things are full of hypocrisy.

Don't dishonor your wife in or out of her presence. When a man doesn't honor his wife he is doing wrong and only hurting himself because the Lord doesn't hear the prayers of evildoers. Marriage doesn't give a man a license to mistreat his woman, it gives him a license to love every inch of that woman. So husbands, be sure to give her the honour and respect. After all she is thy helpmeet; therefore, esteem no one, but God before her and it's God's will that you honour her. As a father you don't want a man to mistreat your daughter but you want him to love her soul. Therefore, understand that you are married to a daughter of God and her Father will get wroth with you, if you dishonor his daughter. The end result of that will not be pretty, so be mindful of how you deal with her. All the windows of heaven will close up on a man that mistreats his woman and his voice will not be heard in the Kingdom. God will take his family from him and give his wife to another MAN. Shame is what a man is promoted if he dishonors his wife

BE MERCIFUL

BLESSED ARE THE MERCIFUL: THEY SHALL OBTAIN MERCY (MATTHEW 5:7)

When a man honours his wife as unto the weaker vessel, he is showing himself to be a merciful man. His heart will not harden when she speaks but he will listen attentively to her. Examples, when a woman tells her husband that she doesn't feel good and doesn't feel like cooking, he should respect what she says and either go cook or go buy them dinner. If he asks her to run into the store with him or for him, and she tells him her feet is hurting from the high heels she's wearing and she prefers to stay in the car, he should respect that and tell her to stay in the car. If she asks him to stop by the store and get something that she needs to go with the dinner, he should respect her. If she needs his assistance with opening things, moving things, carrying things, etc. he should be sure to honour her request. Respect her time and do what she's asks of you and do it as soon as you can. Don't have that selfish and lazy attitude that you'll get to it "whenever" you feel like it, but get off your anal as soon as possible so that she may complete the task at hand. Don't make up excuses why you can't assist her. If the excuses you're giving aren't preventing you from doing and going everywhere else you want to go, such as the gym, club, etc., then it shouldn't be used as an excuse not to honour her request.

A man must also understand that a woman isn't emotionally strong as men so certain things that may not bother him may disturb her. The things that he won't cry about, she might shed many tears over. Knowing these things, a man must be compassionate towards his wife's feelings and emotions. Don't scorn her or insult her character for not being hard like you. Be gentle with her. However, wives, don't think your husband is cold-hearted, if he's not moved by things that you are marinating over. A man must give the utmost respect to his woman, treat her good, listen to her, love her, minister to her and be there for her, because nothing will go right for a man that dishonors his woman. He should give her the affection and attention she needs. He should not make her feel intimidated or that she's in competition with his mother, sister, friends, career, etc. He should always esteem her to be number one in his life. He should involve himself in his wife's business and show her that her business is his business. Never treat her like the challenges that she faces are insignificant or that her issues are unimportant. Therefore, address them and always show your concerns about the issues of her heart, because everything that affects her will affect you. Understand Men, the woman is the one who carries and brings forth precious seed. She is the one who My Lord has created for thy soul to love, and to enjoy. When you honour her, you'll provoke her to want to love you more. You chose her to be your wife, so she should be one of the primary reasons why you labor to build thy house, for she is thy companion and thy glory. The more you love her, the more you'll sow into her, the more you'll honor her, and the more glory you'll receive from her, and if for any reason she despises thee, then sit back, pray for her and let God deal with her, but do your part in maintaining peace in your marriage. The woman being the weaker vessel will be tried tremendously when satanic attacks come against your marriage; the first person the enemy usually assaults is the woman. He wants to use her as bait to cause the man to fall because His ultimate objective is to destroy the man. He knows if he can cause the woman to fall, he can get to the heart of the man, because that is normally where a great portion of a man's heart is. However, a man who has the Word of God hidden in his heart, he understands this and will not lose his integrity when his wife falls short, but he will give himself wholly to God in prayer. He's aware of the enemy's tactic, therefore, he will cleave closer to his wife with the understanding that if he resorts to dishonoring her, it will only weaken their relationship and subject them to more temptations but if he do her right he'll be doing himself a favor.

THE MERICIFUL MAN DOETH GOOD TO HIS OWN SOUL BUT HE THAT IS CRUEL TROUBLETH HIS OWN FLESH (Proverbs.11 17)

CHAPTER FOUR

STOP THE MADNESS

4

STOP THE MADNESS

YET YE SAY WEREFORE? BECAUSE THE LORD HATH BEEN WITNESS BETWEEN THEE AND THE WIFE OF THY YOUTH, AGAINST WHOM THOU HAD DEALT TREACHEROUSLY: YET SHE IS THY COMPANION, AND THE WIFE OF THY COVENANT (Malachi 2:14)

Every man that is dishonoring his wife and has the audacity to cry and complain to God about her and his life, needs to quickly repent and pray for mercy. He needs to examine and correct himself first before he even thinks about addressing her flaws. You cannot be doing wrong outside of the house and wonder why things aren't going right inside of the house. God is not going to let you have it like that. You will reap what you sow; therefore, repent quickly and honor your wife because God is watching you. Men, marriage aren't licenses that grant you the right to treat that woman wrong. When you married her she became your companion and not your slave so don't flip flop on her after she says "I do" and begin to treat her like she's dog manure stuck on the bottom of your shoe. Don't handle her or talk to her like she's a prisoner and you're the warden. She didn't marry you for you to make her feel like she's in bondage to you. As her head, she should respect what you say, but you can't expect for her to submit to you if you're not submitted to Christ. If you want the love of God from her you need to give the love of God to her. We love God because he first loved us, likewise men, that woman should love you because you first loved her. As a man how can you demand respect from her, if you're not respecting her? It's wrong of you to bully her into doing your will, but this is what some men resort to doing believing that violence is the key to controlling their spouse. However, violence shows they have no control over their house. Men stop all forms of abuse, if your wife is being rebellious, pray for her and leave her in God's hands, but whatsoever you do don't lay one finger on her in malice. If you can't love that woman, you don't deserve that woman. Countless of tears have fallen from the eyes of wounded women and the blood of many of them is crying from the ground for justice. Many children suffer greatly from the loss of their mothers and many parents mourn the loss of their daughters who were slaughtered by the hands of men who promised to love them.. What would cause a man to take a bat and bash his wife brains out of her head? What would cause him to take a gun and shoot his woman between her eyes? What would cause a man to douse his wife with gasoline and set her ablaze? What would cause him to take a chainsaw and cut his wife body into pieces? What would cause a man to run over his wife multiple times with his vehicle? What would cause him to take a knife, carve her heart out, roll her body up in carpet and dump her in the river? Those types of horrendous acts don't happen overnight. Normally there are many outrageous and violent acts that led up to that fatal blow so that any woman with an eye to see can see she is walking down deaths row. Anger, rage, jealousy, envy are some of the driving spirits behind these cold blooded murderers which are grounded and rooted in Hatred.

Wives, it's certainly isn't God's will for you to remain in a violent situation. You are in need of deliverance Godspeed. Some people are avid believers that divorce is never the answer, but it's very easy for them to say it because nine times out of ten they are not the ones in the position of getting the brains beat out of them. Getting married doesn't require you to forsake wisdom, if a man is abusing you, be wise and depart from evil. Don't become a fool just because you're married to them. Please pray that God makes you a way out of it.

DELIVER ME, O LORD, FROM THE EVIL MAN: PRESERVE ME FROM THE VIOLENT MAN; WHICH IMAGINE MISCHIEFS IN THEIR HEART; CONTINUALLY ARE THEY GATHERED TOGETHER FOR WAR: THEY HAVE SHARPENED THEIR TONGUE LIKE A SERPENT: ADDERS' POISON IS UNDER THEIR LIPS. SELAH KEEP ME, O LORD, FROM THE HANDS OF THE WICKED: PRESERVE ME FROM VIOLENT MAN; WHO HAVE PURPOSED TO OVERTHROW MY GOINGS (PSALM 140:1-4)

Many women would be alive today had they gotten a divorce, but some of them didn't love themselves enough to let go of what was hurting them. Christ did teach that there should be no divorce saving the cause of fornication; so many believe violence isn't grounds for divorce. However, think about this, if a man doesn't respect you in the house, he surely isn't going to respect you outside of the house and if he hate you enough to physically abuse you, then what's stopping him from having an affair on you, surely it isn't love? If that man is abusing you, you may choose not to divorce him, but by all means SEPARATE yourself from him. A violent man has homicidal tendencies, so wives don't foolishly think that your man only hates you enough to beat you, but he'll never hate you enough to kill you. If he poses any kind of a threat to you, he isn't worthy to be near you. It's better to be divorced and alive than to be killed in a marriage. Many women are covering the altar with tears and crying out to the Lord to either change their abusive husband or to be delivered from him. This should not be the case. The Lord is warning all men to not MISTREAT that woman. She was created for you to love not to hate; therefore, be careful how you entreat her because God is observing your ways with her. He's sees every tear she drops and though God hates divorce he will take that woman away from you.

FOR THE LORD, THE GOD OF ISRAEL, SAITH THAT HE HATETH PUTTING AWAY; FOR ONE COVERETH VIOLENCE WITH HIS GARMENT, SAITH THE LORD OF HOST; THEREFORE TAKE HEED TO YOUR SPIRIT, THAT YE DEAL NOT TREACHEROUSLY. (Malachi 2:14)

SPIRIT OF JEALOUSY

FOR JEALOUSY IS THE RAGE OF MAN HE SHALL NOT SPARE IN THE DAY OF VEAGENCE (PROVERBS 6:34)

Jealousy is one of the main causes of domestic violence and that spirit has plagued and utterly destroyed many households. It has caused the love of many to turn cold and deadly. It is the driving force behind abusive men and women. Many have been killed, hospitalized, and incarcerated because of it. When anyone allow the spirit of jealousy to enter and rest in their heart, their relationship falls into the jaws of hell. Many have murdered their spouse and some has slaughtered their entire family including themselves because of jealousy. Jealousy has caused a man to strangle his wife to death and then take a sharp, knife and carve out of her vagina. Jealousy has caused a woman to take a sharp knife, wait on her husband to fall asleep and proceed to sever his penis off. Jealousy has caused many husbands and wives to war against one another other like gladiators fighting till the death. Depending upon what kind of person a man or woman is, the very thought of their spouse being touched by someone else or having interest in someone else could infuriate them. This kind of jealous spirit has the mindset that says, "I'll kill you before I see you with someone else" also known as **FATAL ATTRACTION**.

Husbands and wives make sure this kind of spirit doesn't abide in you and there are certain indicators that can reveal if that spirit is growing in you. A Jealous person is insecure and fearful. Their mind ponders all kinds of evil thoughts. The slightest thing that doesn't appear right to them, they'll automatically assume the worse and start accusing their spouse. Also, a jealous person doesn't want their spouse to be attractive in no way in the eyes of others because they foolishly believe the less attractive that their spouse is, that no one will else desire them. This exposes how insecure he or she is because in essence, they are saying that they fear their spouse is just that weak and/or whorish of a person, that he or she could possibly sleep with any and/or everyone that desires them. This way of thinking is an absolute insult to the character of spouses that have integrity. If you truly believe your spouse is that wicked of a person, why did you marry him or her? If you're the type of man or woman that doesn't want your spouse to look good, smell good, feel good, do good and prosper in anything that he or she does out of the fear that the more your spouse improves his or herself they won't need you anymore, then you are an insecure and jealous person. If you fear that the more money your spouse earns, he or she won't have any more need of you then your security rest in their poverty and failure, thus you wouldn't support them in anything. You wouldn't want them to better their education, start their own business or do anything that could cause them to earn more money out of fear of losing them. If every time your spouse leaves the house looking good you ask, "Who are you looking good for?" Or if every time your spouse goes to the store you ask, "Who is it at the store that you're trying to impress?" If anytime your spouse goes anywhere you believe they have other intentions beyond the ones they're telling you, you are insecure. Thus the question is why are you insecure? Is it your spouse actions or behavior that causing you to be insecure? Is your spouse flirtatious, dressing provocative, giving more honor to others? Or are you just jealous of your spouse? Are you jealous of your spouse's beauty, success, education? Jealous people are normally always angry, they're always accusing and they have no peace of mind. If this sounds like you, humble yourself and pray. Repent quickly and ask God to purge your heart with His Word. Don't confuse this type of jealousy to be love because love doesn't break you down, it builds you up. Husband and wives if you recognize the spirit of jealousy operating in you, humble yourselves, turn from your wicked waysand pray God cast that spirit out of you. Read and meditate on his word and let him purify your heart by Faith. Bring that spirit of jealousy under subjection, don't let it take control and drive you to harm the one you have profess to love. Whenever you sense jealousy rising up in you, walk away from your spouse before you maliciously cause bodily harm to her or him.

It's foolish for a man or woman to get jealous of the attention their mate receives because your spouse can't control the actions of another person. Don't get mad at them because someone else is showing interest in them. Take it as a compliment because if you were the only person that desires her or him that may indicate you have a mental problem. Understand, if you have a good man or woman, of course others are going to want that person for themselves. So, if you try to keep them down just because you don't want others making advancements towards them, you're not fighting for them but against them. Don't war against your spouse for things he/she has no control over. As long as they handle the situation wisely commend them. Don't make their life with you be as though they are walking on egg shells. How can your spouse relax or feel comfortable talking with you about things, if they feel you'll take everything out of context?

BE YE ANGRY, AND SIN NOT: LET NOT THE SUN GO DOWN UPON YOUR WRATH. (EPHESIANS 4:26)

When a man open his heart to his woman, the type of person that she is determines the issues that enters his life. A real man never wants to think about another person touching his woman. For her body is a restricted area that he holds exclusive rights to. It's a private garden that only he has the benefits of watering, cultivating, touching, and whispering sweetness to her soul; however, if she's a woman that's whorish in her ways, then there will be many heart breaking issues that he would constantly have to deal with. For there are times when a man can feel his woman is too friendly. Although the law of kindness should be on her tongue, that doesn't mean she has to hold conversations with every man that approaches her. The law of kindness does infer that she should reject men who proposition her without being rude, but by using acceptable and inoffensive words. A simple, "Thanks but no thanks, I'm married," shall do.

LOVE AND JEALOUSY

FOR THOU SHALT WORSHIP NO OTHER GOD: FOR THE LORD, WHOSE NAME IS JEALOUS, IS A JEALOUS GOD:(Exodus 24:14)

God himself is Love but he is also a Jealous God. His name is Jealous so anytime you value the things and people that are not of God, more than the things and people that are of God, He gets **WROTH!** He is our creator, our provider, our shepherd, etc. and his love is too good to us, for Him not to get angry with us when we place something or someone above him. His jealousy burns with fury when we as children of God praise another god. His jealousy also ignites when his children praise the wicked over the righteous or when he sees for example, that you are faithful with going to the club every week, but you barely go to church. He gets jealous when you hearken to everyone else's words, but you won't obey his Word. Likewise in Marriage, it's a natural thing for a man or woman who loves their spouse to get jealous, if their made to feel inferior to something or someone else. No husband or wife wants to feel second to anything or anyone but God; therefore, before you accuse your spouse of being jealous or insecure, make sure you're not given him or her reasons to be jealous or insecure. Ask yourself these questions, are you provoking your spouse to jealousy? Men are you choosing to hang out with your friends, in clubs, strips clubs, etc over spending that time with your wife? Are you choosing to masturbate to porn over making love to your wife? No woman or man should feel like their spouse values their friends, sports, the club, kindred, porn etc. more than their marriage. Now a days with so much adultery and homosexuality in this earth, it's natural for a person to become suspect of their spouse if he or she is hanging out with his/her friends more than them? Why should any married person want to hang out in the club without their spouse? And why be at a strip club at all? Environments such as those are catering to sin. Establishments that cater to single men and women dressing provocatively, drinking, and/or bumping and grinding with one another on the dance floor cannot be healthy for a married person to frequent because it often leads to drunkenness and fornication for those who don't have self control.

Too many people that claimed to have loved their spouse wouldn't close their door on certain people, places, or things in their life in order to save and strengthen their marriage. They fought their spouse to hold on to those things or people and it cost them their marriage, which proves they valued those things over their marriage. Your ex is your ex for a reason, so there is no need for your EX to be in your life, unless you have kids with her or him. If you're not discussing the kids with your Ex, then you don't need to be discussing anything with your Ex. Your spouse is there to make love to you, so there's no need for you to masturbate to porn. In order to guard your marriage you must close those doors on all people, places, and things that are distractions and weapons the enemy is using against it. Think about this: If that person, place, or thing is that important to you that you are willing to sacrifice the peace in your marriage to hold on to it, then you should have married that person, place or thing. However, If you want to save your marriage, CLOSE THE DOOR and stop putting the world before your Marriage.

LOVE NOT THE WORLD, NEITHER THE THINGS THAT ARE IN THE WORLD, IF ANY MANY LOVE THE WORLD, THE LOVE OF THE FATHER IS NOT IN HIM(1 JOHN 2:15)

MAN OR MONSTER

SO OUGHT MEN TO LOVE THEIR WIVES AS THEIR OWN BODIES. HE THAT LOVETH HIS WIFE LOVETH HIMSELF FOR <u>NO MAN YET HATED HIS OWN FLESH</u>; BUT NOURISH AND CHERISHETH IT, EVEN AS THE LORD THE CHURCH (EPHESIANS 5:29)

Husbands are you a Man or a Monster? The answer to this question is made known by how you treat your woman. If you are patient with her, spending quality time with her, enjoying her, completely honest with her, nurturing her, providing for her, praying for her, loving her in deed and in truth, sowing and watering her with the Word of God, concerned about her all the issues of her heart, making love to her, etc. then you are A Man. As a man you should protect her with your life, knowing that the way you love your wife reveals how much you love yourself. On the other hand, if you are abusing her in any form, if you are reviling, lying, deceitful, selfish, and careless and causing her pain, then you are a Monster because NO MAN has ever hated his own flesh. A Man understands that a woman was created for Him and he will never hate what God created for him to love. However, a monster has not this understanding being that he has a diabolical mind. He is animalistic in nature and governed by strange cravings. He only seeks to gratify his vile affections upon a woman. Many wives have become victims of brutality and homicide because they made the mistake of marrying a monster. Some of these monsters deceived them by wearing the disguise of a man in the beginning and the costume wasn't removed until after they said I DO and thus, these women found themselves trapped in the snares of death. They mistook lust to be love and shortly after marrying him, their eyes was immediately opened to who they said, "I DO" TO.

I SAID IN MINE HEART CONCERNING THE ESTATE OF THE SONS OF MEN, THAT GOD MIGHT <u>MANIFEST</u> THEM, AND THAT THEY MIGHT SEE THAT THEY THEMSELVES ARE <u>BEASTS</u>. (ECCLESIASTES 3:18)

Men, if you're behaving like a school yard pimp or an one eyed slave master towards your woman, God despise that image of the monster that you are. Open your eyes and recognize that you are not a man. Your behavior deems you unworthy of a woman. Your wife needs the love of a man not the rage of a beast. She shouldn't have to file for an order of protection on the man that supposes to protect her. Many women never thought the man that they marred would hurt or kill them. Though some of the signs were evident "before" marriage, they either chose to either ignore it or they had a strange attraction to violent men. However, they later learned that you cannot get the right kind of love out of the wrong kind of man. The ears of a woman should never have to hear her man call her derogatory names. Even if he claims to have spoken those things out of anger, it's no excuse because a woman shouldn't have to struggle with trying to figure out if he truly meant those things that he said. When a man speaks in a hateful manner, he's robbing his wife of the peace she needs to feel secure in the marriage with him. How can a woman feel like her man will be true to her, when he's making her feel like she means nothing to him? How can she feel that he value her presence in his life, when he's talking to her like she isn't worth the spit on the bottom of his shoe? Men if your calling your wife a b**** or a Whore and you honestly believe she fits that profile, why are you married to her? And if you don't believe she fits that profile, why refer to her as that? The character of the male you are is revealed in your words. A man won't refer to his woman as a dog, but a monster will. Men if you fit the profile of a monster, repent immediately and wives if your husband is a monster, PRAY because

Whoso is partner with a thief hateth his own soul: he heareth cursing, and bewrayeth it not. (Proverbs 29:24)

THE BRAWLER

FOR THREE THINGS THE EARTH IS DISQUIETED, AND FOR FOUR WHICH IT CANNOT BEAR: ....FOR AN ODIOUS WOMAN WHEN SHE IS MARRIED; AND A HANDMAID THAT IS HEIR TO HER MISTRESS. (PROVERBS (30:21,23)

Women, it takes more than having a vagina to be a wife, so understand that just because you're a female, that doesn't mean you're qualified to be a wife. Some men rushed to judgment and were deceived by the beauty and/or charisma of certain females, and unfortunately they found themselves married to a beast. Wives examine your ways and be certain that you're not a woman that's full of strife and debate. Do you argue, fuss and fight with your man daily? Are you a brawling woman? The Spirit of rage possesses brawling women causing them to be quick to snap on their man. They will throw anything at a man they can get their hands on. They'll intentionally do things to humiliate him, such as make a scene in public places, key up his car, kick through his windshield, flatten his tires, cut and burn up his clothes, dig their nails in his flesh in an effort to scar up his body, etc.. They'll be screaming so loudly in the house, that those outside of the house, would believe that her husband must be in the house violating them, yet he may not be doing anything wrong. These women are verbally and physically abusive. Wives this should not be the case, but if it is, recognize that the enemy is using you and repent, because God created you to be a woman not a beast. Therefore check yourself, knowing that it's not becoming of a woman to behave like a raging bull. Every woman needs to be loved, but a brawling woman is an out of control beast that needs to be tamed.

A brawling woman cannot appreciate the love of a man. She will take his kindness for weakness and falsely accuse him of not being strong enough to handle her, just because he won't stoop to acting ignorant like her. A brawling woman will say things that will cause a man to feel as though he's been hit with a ton a bricks, such as: She can sleep with his family or friends, she'll tell him his children aren't his, she'll tell him she hates him, etc. She speaks

93

and does things that provoke her man to smack the taste out of her mouth, but "husbands" don't even think about it. Regardless of how this woman tempts you to fight her, be man enough to walk away from her. The brawling woman has the potential to kill and some of them have murdered their husband. If they didn't murder him manually, the stress that some of them have inflicted, caused their husband's to kill them. In the beginning the woman was never made to be the cause of a man's death, but she was created to make a man's life worth living. The Creation of the Woman was God bringing life to man, not him taking life away from man.

Genesis 3:20 And Adam called his wife's name Eve; because she was the mother of all living.

EVE
Original: *חוה*
Transliteration: *chavvâh*
Phonetic: *khav-vaw'*
BDB Definition: Eve = " life" or " living"
the first woman, wife of Adam

Eve's name in Hebrew means Life or Living and when the woman understands the essence of who she is and where she came from, she'll understand how powerful she is. Wives you were created to bring life into A Man's world and this is why it was not good for man to be alone, because man wouldn't see life worth living without her.

Females that are ignorant of who they are have a very poor self image. These are the kind of females that A MAN can't live with because they are carnal minded, liking to brawl and by no means are they pleasing in the eyes of God. Their tongue is as a bitter sword that will cut a man to his core. They act animalistic in nature, some even stoop so low that they call themselves sluts, hoes, and B****. Instead of being a blessing in their man's life, they will ruin his life.

Romans 8:6-8 For to be carnally minded is death; but to be spiritually minded is life and peace.7 Because the carnal mind is enmity against God: for it is not subject to the law of God, neither indeed can be.8 So then they that are in the flesh cannot please God.

A man has no peace with a brawling woman, being that she is an odious woman, which means she is hateful. The earth itself is enraged when this kind of woman gets married, so one can only imagine the hell she puts her husband through. He gets no glory from her. The way she treats him is despicable. Her fits of rage will tear the whole house down and afterwards, she'll be confident that she has done nothing wrong. This woman has homicidal tendencies because her actions are deadly. For Example, she'll start punching her man while he is driving on the highway. She'll throw knives, pots and pans at him, key his car and slash her man's tires, rip up his clothes, burn up his belongings, and spread all kinds of lies on him. She'll pull out a gun on him. She is full of hypocrisy; and will berate her husband in front of others. Anyone who gives ear to her, will be deceived to believe that her husband is the villain in their relationship, because of the bad picture she paints of him. And to top it all off she'll have the audacity to wonder why his family doesn't like her.

Any man that is married to this type of woman needs to separate himself from her, go into deep prayer and seek God's guidance. If you're not the type of man that will physically fight her back, she'll surely accuse you of being a weak man that's unable to control her and if you are the type of man that will fight her back, it only enrages her more. Regardless of what that woman has done or said to get under your skin, don't war with her carnally by no means. If she resorts to acting violent with you, restrain her in self defense, but don't you dare fight her like she's another man. Afflict no bodily harm upon her. If or whenever she starts acting bananas on you, always be man enough to walk away from her! Understand that the best thing you can do for you and her, is to pray for her and stay away from her until she gets her act together.

It is better to dwell in a corner of the housetop, than with a →brawling woman← in a wide house. (Proverbs 21:9)

Wives, if you don't want to lose your husband's repent from that foolishness and be God's definition a wife to your husband because a man needs you to be a GOOD THING.

A MAN NEEDS A WOMAN

And the LORD God said, It is not good that the man should be alone; I will make him a "help meet" for him. (Genesis 2:18)

Women that know who they are in Christ are the ones that A MAN can't live without, because they are spiritually minded, thus, they see themselves the way God created them to be and walk accordingly. They understand they were made to love the Soul of a man and they enrich his world. Wives, understand the way you love the soul of a man is by doing what God made the woman to be, which is a Help Meet for her man. Help means to assist, encourage, motivate, support, strengthen, serve, aid, etc. so a woman should support a man in every facet of his life, be it physically, financially, and emotionally. She shouldn't do his work for him, but be a help to him because the divine purpose of the woman is to be there for her man. Because of her his life should be better not worse off.

In the beginning, one of the greatest acts of love that God performed on Adam was making him a WOMAN. Although God had already given the man power, purpose, pets, the world etc. he understood that A MAN can have all of those things, but yet none of those things could provide him companionship, affection, friendship, nourish him, make him happy, or make life meaningful to him. He also understood that although a man may love those things, none of those things could give him that love in return and this is why A MAN needs A WOMAN because without the Love of woman, a man wouldn't find life worth living. Any man that feels as though he doesn't need a woman is not a man. A MAN knows that the woman was created by God FOR HIM!!

Neither was the man created for the woman; but the woman "for" the man. (1 Corinthians 11:9)

Before God made Man the woman, in the scriptures below we see that although Adam had the whole world in the palm of his hand, he was still searching for more subconsciously.

And out of the ground the LORD God formed every beast of the field, and every fowl of the air; and brought them unto Adam to see what he would call them: and whatsoever Adam called every living creature that was the name thereof. 20 And Adam gave names to all cattle, and to the fowl of the air, and to every beast of the field; but for Adam there was not "found" an help meet for him.(Genesis 2:19,20)

As God brought Adam all the creatures of the earth to name, consciously or subconsciously he was looking amongst them for something that was "agree-able" to him. He was hoping to find someone that resemble him from the inside-out. Someone cut from the same fabric having his same style. Someone he could share and exchange thoughts with, someone that understood and saw the world as he saw it. Someone who spoke his language walked the way he walked, and could live the way he lived. Someone he could laugh and enjoy the presence of God and all of the creation with, a special someone that would strengthen and motivate him while he's doing the will of God. Someone who, respects, honors, cares and tends to him, as he tends to fulfilling God's purpose for him, because a "A Man " without that "someone" is alone. Wives be that someone for your husband because if you're not that someone to him, he'll still feel alone even while he's married to you.

When a man feels alone there's a sense of emptiness within him. He'll feel that there's a void in him that needs to be filled. You could be lying next to him every night, but he'll feel like he's disconnected and far away from you. It will seem as if he's in this world all by himself. It's a bad thing for a "Man" to be alone because in the process of time it could bring depression, anxieties, frustrations, and mixed emotions upon him. In order to fill the void many have resorted to sin which only deepened their void. A man that is alone cannot bring forth the good fruits of love, joy, and peace within himself, so that he may feel good about himself; therefore, God fearfully wonderfully made something beautiful for the man. He created him a woman and the woman God created for man was not a sister, mother, or a daughter, but she was his Wife, a help meet for him. So the kind of Love that a Man needs to fill a certain void can only be supplied through A Wife. God didn't make another male, animal, or a toy for the man nor do they have the ability to provide the kind of love a man needs. God made man a woman, so wives be the Woman your man needs.

So God created man in his own image, in the image of God created he him; male and "female" created he them. (Genesis 1:27)

Wives, walk in the image that God originally created you to walk in, which is Love. Love is the perfection of beauty, so walking in the love of Christ is what makes you a beautiful woman inside and out. Before sin entered the world and corrupted the image of man, the hearts of men were created pure, so the woman could think no evil, say no evil, nor do any evil to her man. She gave him the utmost respect and honored him. She was a blessing to his soul in every way because LOVE was innately in her. When a woman loves a man "the way" God originally designed her to, she strengthens him, she speaks life into him and she caters to him. She makes him feel important to her. Anything he needs her to do, she does it joyfully. She understands "who" she is and her place as a woman; therefore, she doesn't challenge, compete, or go against him, but submits to him because she knows she was made for him. His wants and needs are a priority to her. She understands that God uses her to pour out his love on him; therefore, her man is never without the companionship, compassion, and affection he needs. She makes him feel good about him being "the man" that God created him to be. Wives, you are the one who are supposed to be a Help meet for your husband, so provide him the love that he needs from you. Also pray for understanding, because the Love of God resides inside a prudent woman.

House and riches are the inheritance of fathers and a "prudent wife" is from the LORD.(Proverbs 19:14)

Heaven won't send a man a foolish woman, but this explains why some men are living in hell, because they married to women that are not equipped with the wisdom to love them. The spirit of these women aren't right with God, so his Love isn't flowing through them. Wives if you want your marriage to last, in all thy getting get understanding, so that you can be all of the woman that man needs handling all thy matters wisely.

SECURE EACH OTHER'S HEART

ABSTAIN FROM ALL APPEARANCES OF EVIL (1Th5:22

The heart is the most vital part of the body. Not only physically but spiritually also, physically because regardless to what part of your body gets injured, as long as you have a heartbeat you're alive, and you have time to healed and made whole again. If your heart ever stops beating, the blood stops flowing and your time in this life has expired. The heart is spiritually important because whenever My Lord plants a seed in us, he plants it in our hearts, which washes and purifies our heart and bring forth the fruits of righteousness; therefore, the enemy tries his best to snatch the seed out of our hearts and to pollute it with sin. My Lord commands that we keep our hearts with all diligence because out of our heart flows the issues of life. We must watch what we allow into our heart, that we not give our hearts to the wrong person. Love all people, but guard thy heart. Always observe a person's ways, and if you notice they are a hazard, lock your heart up. Never open your heart in an unsafe environment. Husbands and wives should be a safe and pleasant environment to one another.

When your heart isn't secure it will be very easy for the enemy to start confusion in your marriage because there isn't any trust established. If your spouse can't trust you, it will lead them to question everything you do out of fear of being betrayed or getting their heart broken by you. Whenever things don't appear right on your end, it could cause them to rush to judgment and make false accusations against you. Though he or she may be wrong in what their accusing you of, you must put yourself in their position and see how it looks through their eyes and if it doesn't look right, be understandable as to why they are accusing you of it. If you care anything about them, don't have that, "I don't care what you think," attitude about the situation. You can't respond to the situation with, "You can think whatever you want to think," because if it appears that you are wrong, then in their mind YOUR GUILTY until proven innocent. Be compassionate towards their feelings because they have every right to feel the way they feel until you do whatever it takes to clean up the mess.

Please understand the power of perception and avoid all appearances of evil. By avoiding those appearances you won't grant Satan the opportunity to have a field day in your spouse's mind. When things do happen that was completely out of your control and that doesn't appear right, never take on that careless or cold attitude as if you don't need to prove anything to your spouse. If you love him or her whether they ask you to or not, you should take it upon yourself to eliminate confusion. Do whatever is within your power to prove that things are not what they appear to be. In doing so, the situation that the enemy tried to use to come in-between you two, will in-turn strengthen you two. For example, while a man and his wife are asleep, they are awakened by the vibrations of her cell phone at 2 a.m., and he wants to know who is that calling or texting her in the wee hours of the morning. To remove all curiosity, she simply hands him her phone so that he may see for himself. Had she done what most cheaters do, which is immediately say it was one of her girlfriends or relatives and erase all her texts and call log history before allowing him to see her phone, contentions would have transpired between them.

Satan has destroyed many relationships by making something appear to be something it was not because perception is powerful. He knows that men judge by appearance. So although you may not be cheating on your spouse, the enemy does all that he can to make it appear as though you are cheating, in hopes of rumors and lies getting back to your spouse. If he can put you in situations where it appears as though you're being unfaithful the more powerful his forged lies will be. Another Example, a married woman spends many of her lunches and breaks with one of her male co-workers. Rumors quickly spread on the job that they are having an affair and her spouse hears about this affair through one of his cousins who has a friend that works for the same company as his wife. He already doesn't trust his wife because of previous things that have happened that didn't look right, so he immediately starts questioning and accusing her of sleeping with her co-worker. Instead of her being understanding of why he is upset, she gets offended because in her mind she hasn't done anything wrong, she just seems to get along better with him than with her female co workers. However in her husband's mind, since there are many cases in which co-workers do have affairs with each other, which could very well be the case with his wife, he doesn't accept any excuse that she gives him. In his opinion, she has no business going to lunch with no man unless it's work related.

In order to eliminate confusion and prevent lies from manifesting married men and women need to avoid these types of situations. Knowing that men judge by outward appearance, whenever situations develop that appear twisted, couples should be willing to go the extra mile and provide whatever proof necessary, that brings clarity to them. Think of those situations as being good opportunities to establish trust between one another, so that when things do occur that don't appear right and that you can't provide any proof for, hopefully enough trust would have been earned, that you'll be quicker to give each other the benefit of the doubt. It's much easier to take someone's word and extend them credit after they've established a good track record of being honest.

Secure means a protected and safe place that is free from danger or the risk of being harmed or stolen. Husband and wives above all things, pray fervently for wisdom and become that safe-haven your spouse needs for you to be. Wisdom will direct you on how to take care of each other's heart. Any man or woman with the wisdom to secure their spouse's heart will never break their spouse's heart. Securing your spouse's heart gives her or him the blessed assurance their heart needs in order for it to trust in you. When the heart is secure, your spouse will feel more comfortable pouring out all his or hers heart to you, because they'll know that their secrets are safe with you. Therefore, his or her heart is hidden from pain, sorrow and hell, being that you're a good caretaker of it. Regardless of how bad situations become, you'll never make your spouse feel like it's a burden for you to love him or her because you love loving him or her.

Some ways to secure each other's heart:

1. Always speak the truth regardless of how disappointing it could be and if you lie in haste, immediately confess the truth, don't let your spouse find out through some other means that you lied.

2. Never act ashamed to be seen with your spouse or be unwilling to take your spouse anywhere with you without a valid reason.

3. Always be understanding of one another. If any pain has been inflicted, medicate the pain you or someone else has caused them with acts of compassion. Don't deepen their wound with a careless attitude, but be responsive to one another needs.

4. Always encourage, and pray for one another.

5. Don't provoke one another to jealousy. Don't act as though you value your relationship with your parents, kids, friends, pets, job, material possessions, or club more than your spouse.

6. Don't ever act like you have something to hide. Your spouse should always be allowed to answer your cell phone, go through your personal stuff, etc.

7. Answer the phone whenever you know your spouse is calling

you. If you can't answer, make sure you quickly return the call, and be willing to explain why and/or your whereabouts. Don't act as though you don't owe her or him any explanations.

8. Avoid all appearances of evil. Don't open up any doors for Satan to speak.

9. Always give each other the utmost respect and honor. Never speak evil or against each other. When conflict arises quickly resolve the issue, forgive one another, and be tenderhearted towards each other. Always make peace as quickly as possible.

10. Don't flirt or give no one else a reason to think you have interest in them.

11. Love one another which is the fulfilling of the law

A God fearing man or woman will never do anything that gives their spouse a reason to feel insecure, but If you hear yourself always asking the question, "If you love me how could you...?", and if they can't give you good understanding as to why, to clear up your conscious, then obviously your spouse is doing things to make you feel insecure. For example, so many married men and woman have accounts with online dating sites and some of them have been caught indulging in inappropriate conversations. Some have been caught chatting going down memory lane with their first love from high school and after he or she gets exposed they have the audacity to call their spouse insecure, as though they don't have a very good reason to be. When you are married what's your purpose of being online meeting people or reuniting with your ex? Your spouse can't feel secure with you. Their soul can't find rest in you because your actions are causing them to question your loyalty to them. Stop playing games and do all you can do to protect your marriage. You should get offended by anyone who proceeds to test you after you've made it clear that you're married, because that person is not only disrespecting you and your spouse, but their also disrespecting God. It also reveals what type of man or woman they think or hope that you are, because only a person with whorish ways, will have an affair on his or her spouse. So don't exchange numbers, emails, or give the enemy any kind of means of contacting you. Here are some techniques that you can do to ward off some your tempters.

WEAR YOUR RING

In America's Culture wedding rings and bands are indicators that you are married. So if you are married why wouldn't you want to wear your ring? Why wouldn't you want people to know that you are married? If you leave the house with your ring on, but when you return home your ring is off, then of course that alone will raise your spouse's eyebrow. Unless you work a job that prohibits you from wearing jewelry, there's no excuse for you not to wear your ring. The wedding ring is a beautiful way to make a strong statement to others that you are off the market without you having to say one mumbling word. The size, design and value of the ring doesn't reflect ones faithfulness to their spouse, because a person can break their vows with or without a band, nor does a wedding ring reflect the quality of the love and strength of one's marriage. However, they are powerful in deterring many from approaching you that would have otherwise tried to get to know you, had you not had on a ring. This is why some singles wear wedding rings that they may give off the perception of being marred in hopes of fanning off unwanted attention. Some will approach you in-spite of the ring, but in those cases all you should have to do is flash the ring and say yes it's true that you're married and your true it. If after your marital status is made clear to them and they continue to be persistent in their pursuit of you, then behold the devil because only a devil will covet another man's wife or husband.

WALK WISELY

Lies are powerful. They have →utterly destroyed←many relationships, marriages, and lives; therefore, if you value what you have its important that you walk wisely or you will lose what you got. Understand some people weren't guilty of the crime they were convicted of, but they were guilty of putting themselves in →the position to be falsely accused of it.

Example, if a woman visits a male friend of hers and that man decided to lie on his penis and tell all his associates he slept with her, and her Man "hears" of it. More than likely He's not going to believe His woman when she denies the accusations because she probably wouldn't be able to give "proof" that she's speaking the truth and many questions will be raised in his head such as:

1. WHY would she be there in the FIRST PLACE?

2. What was her true intentions for going?

3. If she didn't have Sex "WHAT" did she do?

4. And if she didn't do anything, again WHY GO to his house?

5. If the guy is lying. then why she wasn't wise enough to see the type of man this fool was? Therefore, either she didn't know him long enough or she has poor judgment in character, so either way you want to look at it, in his eyes she royally MESSED UP!!

He surely isn't going to believe all they did was pray and read the bible. Simply because she foolishly went to his house she gave the devil the OPPORTUNITY to bring mass confusion into her relationship. Too many people Lie & Cheat so you can't expect for a person to trust you if your do things that appear like you cheated; therefore, If you want to secure what you have, walk wisely and don't put yourself in the position to be lied on or SET UP!!

In Conclusion, understand cheaters-->always<-- do things that don't appear right and they always have EXCUSES (Lies) for it. If you question or don't accept their excuse they are quick to call you jealous or insecure in efforts to shift the blame on you. That's one of Satan's methods to deceive you and cause you to question your own intelligence by making it appear as though you're the one causing the problems in the relationship. Truth is, no one's heart can feel secure with someone who is doing things that doesn't look right. If you care about your man or woman's peace of mind one of the steps in securing his or her heart is to

ABSTAIN FROM ALL APPEARANCES OF EVIL
(1Thessolonians 5:22)

THE CONDUCT OF LOVE

LOVE DOTH NOT BEHAVE ITSELF UNSEEMLY...(1 CORINTHIANS 13: 5)

One day a woman who was married to her husband for 16yrs, went though his cell phone and found pictures of him receiving oral sex from another man and her whole world was crushed. Up until that day she thought she had a wonderful man, but now she had to accept that fact that through the course of her entire journey with him she had been living a lie. Upon discovering the truth, her mind immediately flashed back to everyone that has ever told her that they felt her husband had a little sugar in his tank. She honestly thought they were just jealous and hating on her relationship, but comes to find out they were speaking the truth. She wondered how long she had been looking like a plain fool because on the surface her husband was good to her leaving behind no clue of his vile nature. Had he been walking in the Love of God and loved his wife sincerely, there's no way he would have behaved in such indecent way and brought upon her such disgrace. A Husband that behaves himself unseemly may FEEL he love his wife, but he doesn't Love her at all!

Many define Love as a mindless emotion, but Love brings you joy. However, love means so much than just a good sensation. Love has a code of conduct; therefore, there are certain things love just won't do. Love is not immoral, so if the Love of God is flowing through you, you won't behave yourself in any kind of way that would bring hurt, embarrassment and shame upon yourself nor the ones you love because love doesn't behave itself unseemly. Love beautifies you; therefore, the way you carry yourself and everything thing you do, not only will it make you look very attractive, but the ones you love will look good also because the things you'll do for them will be a blessing to their soul and they'll look foolish if they ever let you go! Your husband or wife will walk with the confidence of knowing that he or she has a good mate because your love isn't behaving disorderly, thus, it's not causing them any disgrace.

If your behavior is embarrassing, If it's causing them to look like a fool for being with you, then you're not loving them. Example, If you showing your anal in public, if your being disrespectful by flirting with others behind their back, if you're doing anything, be it openly or in secret that's making your spouse LOOK STUPID, you're not walking in the Spirit of love because Love doesn't act like that!

SEEK NOT YOUR OWN

BLESSED IS THE MAN THAT WALKETH NOT IN THE COUNSEL OF THE UNGODLY, NOR STANDETH IN THE WAY OF SINNERS, NOR SITTEH IN THE SEAT OF THE OF TH SCORNFUL. BUT HIS DELIGHT IN THE LAW OF THE LORD: AND HIS LAW DOTH HE MEDITATE DAY AND NIGHT. AND HE SHALL BE LIKE A TREE PLANTED BY THE RIVERS OF WATER, THAT BRINGETH FORTH HIS FRUIT IN HIS SEASON; AND HIS LEAF ALSO SHALL NOT WITHER; AND WHATSOEVER HE DOETH PROSPER (PSALMS 1:1)

One of the keys to having a blessed marriage is to not give ear to the advice of ungodly people, but to make sure you give your mind and heart to the Word of God. If you commit thy ways unto the Lord your marriage shall be grounded and nourished with everything its needs to produce good fruit. Don't make the mistake that many have made and follow the suggestions of those who have no fear of God. The impact of their advice will only be damaging to your relationship. Bottom line, stop listening to people and hearken to the voice of God.

A woman wanted to surprise her husband for his Birthday with something different. She spoke to a coworker who suggest giving her husband a threesome, she was adamantly against it, but after talking to others who encourage her to do it, her curiosity was peaked, so her mind began to change on the issue. Without making it known to her husband, she decided to surprise him with a threesome for his birthday. She got a bi-sexual attractive woman who happened to be that same co worker that encouraged her to try it. On this particular day when her husband came home, he walked inside his bedroom and discovered two beautiful women lying naked in his bed. He eyes lit up like a Christmas tree, He ripped of his clothes, took a quick shower and dove right in between the lanes. All of them maximized the moment together. What the couple didn't know was, that moment of radical pleasure was about to revolutionize their life because immediately after the dark session had ended, the husband looked at his wife differently. His respect for her was lost and within a few months he filed for divorce because he no longer perceived her to be an honorable woman. This woman's biggest mistake is that she followed the desire of her own heart when it came to pleasing her husband, instead of hearkening to the commandment of God. What she thought would fortify and strengthen her marriage actually destroyed her marriage. Had this woman obeyed the commandment of God, she would not have fulfilled the evil desires of her own heart and her marriage could still be alive and well!!

And it shall be unto you for a fringe, that ye may look upon it, and remember all the commandments of the LORD, and do them; and that ye seek →not after your own heart← and your own eyes,← after which ye →use to go a whoring:(Numbers 15:39)

God made his people wear fringes on their garments for constants reminders to obey his Word and not their own will. Men and women learn from this. They need to cease from looking at TEMPTATIONS and keep their eyes on the Word of the Lord. The need to frame the commandments of God on the wall, post them on their desk at work, hang tassels in their car etc.

as a reminder to obey the commandment of God because many marriages have fallen due to them following the lust of their eyes and the wicked imaginations of their own heart. That lust has driven many into a world of adultery and whoredom. A good example of this error, is when couples are seeking ways to SPICE UP their marriage and their own heart suggest ways of doing so by fantasizing of threesomes, orgies, swinging and other forms of perversion as methods to spicing it up. The commandment of God instructs us not to commit fornications and adultery, but those things tempt us to do the exact opposite. As enticing to the eyes and flesh those things may be to you, it's not wise to indulge in those forbidden pleasures because the aftermath of those moments of sinful gratification is a lot of pain. Understand if you follow your heart and/or eyes it can lead you down many wrong paths, so if you want your relationship to be built to last, you must fear God and don't participate in activities that will destroy the foundation. Don't let your heart or eyes lead you in way that are contrary to love's code of conduct because LOVE seeks not her own will but the will of God.

Doth not behave itself unseemly, SEEK NOT HER OWN,← is not easily provoked, thinketh no evil; (1 Corinthians 13:5)

NOT INFRONT OF THE KIDS

And did not he make one? Yet had he the residue of the spirit. And wherefore one? That he might seek a godly seed← Therefore take heed to your spirit, and let none deal treacherously against the wife of his youth. (Malachi 2:15)

Many women and men have remained in abusive situations for the sake of their children, but if your children are being exposed to you two acting a fool with one another, then it's not good for them for you two to remain together. Men you are the head of the house. You set the tone; therefore, put your foot down and be the living example of Love. Your kids shouldn't be exposed to cursing, hatred and violence so repent from it. If your wife is acting like your enemy, love her as your enemy and render good for evil. Pray for wisdom that you may handle every matter wisely. Understand, you need to raise your children in a loving and peaceful environment and establish the premise for them to live by. Kids are easily influenced; many young men don't respect women because that example was never set forth for them. They never saw their father love their mother, so they grow up with a "we don't love these hoes" mentality. So, how can you expect a young man to know how to love a woman when He never SAW IT in action? Nor can he learn from his Father if his father is missing in action. He won't know how to be the man of the house if he saw his mother wear the pants in the house. He won't know how to treat his woman as queen, if all he saw was his father treat his mother like a dog. Likewise, many women don't respect men because their mother was a very poor example of a wife. They witness their mother being rebellious towards their father, so many of them grew up with the mindset that a man can't tell them what to do, which doesn't produce a meek and quiet spirit in them. Other women saw their mother tolerate being disrespected by their father, thus, believing if a man doesn't act a fool with her that man must not love her. How can you expect a woman to know how a man should love her, if she never saw her Father love her mother? Parents you may have given your kids the example of what not to do but where do they get the example of what to do from?

In conclusion, husband and wives, if love was the reason you married one another then why are you behaving like you hate one another? God made you one that you may be fruitful (Loving) and multiple. He wants you to produce godly children not "hell hounds," but when you're acting like devils and raising your children in a hostile household, you more than likely going to produce two fold more the children of hell, than yourselves. When kids witness their parents cursing and fighting one another like hellhounds, they grow up believing malicious behavior is an expression of true Love. On the other hand, real love becomes a strange incomprehensible thought in the figment of their imaginations! PARENTS learn how to Love, that you may be the example of love for kids to follow, that they may grow into loving human beings and not monsters.

TRAIN UP A CHILD IN THE WAY HE SHOULD GO: ANDWHEN HE IS OLD, HE WILL NOT DEPART FROM IT. (Proverbs 22:6)

CHAPTER FIVE

LOVE MAKING

5

LOVE MAKING

Adam KNEW Eve his Wife, and she conceived, and bare can, and said I have begotten a man from the LORD.(Genesis 4:1)

When Adam knew his wife, it meant that he made love to her. Knew means to discover, to know by experience, became acquainted with her. Therefore, whenever a man makes love to his wife he is exploring and discovering her. He is learning her through experience. That experience is so powerful that is has the ability to procreate life. Those who don't understand the Essence and Value of it but only seek to enjoy the pleasure of it, turns that experience that was meant to be sanctified, pure and beautiful into something dirty, nasty, sinful by practicing it outside of marriage. Christ taught those that have sex outside of marriage commits fornication and defile their bodies.

Matthew 15:19 For out of the heart proceed evil thoughts, murders, adulteries, FORNICATIONS, thefts, false witness, blasphemies:20 These are the things which DEFILE a Man: but to eat with unwashen hands defileth not a man.

Fornications
G4202
Original: πορνεία
Transliteration: porneia
Phonetic: por-ni'-ah
Thayer Definition:
illicit sexual intercourse
adultery, fornication, homosexuality, lesbianism, intercourse with animals etc.
sexual intercourse with close relatives; Lev. 18
sexual intercourse with a divorced man or woman;

Fornications according to its biblical definition is adultery, homosexuality, bestiality, incest, etc.. fornication is unlawful lust that covers a variety of sins. It's sex outside of marriage and these are sins committed against your body and believers are commanded to FLEE from them because they DEFILE YOU. Your body is a holy temple, so don't treat it like a house of harlots because in doing so, you destroy your temple. This is one of the reasons why marriage is very important, especially to those who can't control their lust. Although it's a good thing to remain single and serve the Lord without any distraction, however, as the scripture saith below,

NEVERTHELESS TO AVOID FORNICATION, LET EVERY MAN HAVE HIS OWN WIFE, AND LET EVERY WOMAN HAVE HER OWN HUSBAND. LET THE HUSBAND RENDER UNTO THE WIFE DUE BENEVOLENCE: AND LIKEWISE THE WIFE UNTO THE HUSBAND. (1CORINTHIANS 7:2-3)

When speaking of marriage, you are speaking of an exclusive relationship between a man and his woman that's been sealed by God. It is a commitment between two people who have vowed to God to give their bodies solely to one another and God will hold them accountable to it. The Lord oversees the operations of the relationship and he has set a golden rule that husbands and wives must give each other due love (sex). Your bodies become one in marriage; therefore, God's definition of sex is experienced in Marriage because when you understand what Sex is through the eyes of God, you understand the importance of waiting until you get married to have sex because sex outside of marriage isn't sex, its sin(fornications). Sex within marriage is LOVE MAKING and it's the greatest deed of love shared between two people that has been bonded together by the hand of God. It's a form of communication called body language that reveals you're deepest desires for your spouse allowing him or her to explore places inside of you that only they have access to.

God instructs husband and wives to give one another due benevolence. Benevolence means goodwill and kindness, so sex in marriage is a show of kindness and 1ˢᵗ Corinthians 13:4 teach us that LOVE is KIND. Therefore, if you're married, you OWE your spouse that LOVE. Pay them what you OWE them. Husbands and wives should never hold out on one another. You don't get married to not make love but to make love. If you're not going to have sex, there's no need to get married. Two people can be friends, love and be there for one another; financially, mentally, and spiritually and do everything that married couples do, outside having sex and it wouldn't be a sin. However, what sanctifies marriage is that the day you say I DO, you have declared to God that your love has grown to the point that you want to spend the rest of your life with her or him, and that your desire has reached the point that you can no longer contain the fire in your soul that is burning to be one in body with her or him.

Lovemaking is a beautiful thing and husbands and wives need to make love to one another as often as possible because it's the deepest and kindest expression of love you can give to them, that no one else can give them. Lovemaking is part of the Marital lifestyle, so if you're not making love, unless there's a medical reason that preventing you from doing so, then what differentiates your marriage from any other relationship? Let's not be deceived because it takes much more than love making to maintain a healthy marriage. If you don't fulfill the other duties that love requires of you such as faithfulness, communication, consistency, respect, honor, honesty, time, prayer, good deeds, patience, provision, etc. you are fallen short and that could cause your spouse to lose his or her desire for you. Those other things that you are not doing are the essentials needed to produce a healthy, strong, and lasting marriage but you cannot leave sex out of it. Figuratively speaking, Jesus exposed the hypocrisy of the Jews who paid tithes, but they didn't obey the more important things in the law. Paying the tithe may have kept them in good standing with the Pastor and the Church, but the things they weren't doing didn't keep them in right standing with God.

SCRIBES, PHARISEES, YE HYPOCRITES, FOR <u>YE PAY TITHE</u> OF MINT AND ANISE AND CUMMIN, AND HAVE <u>OMITTED</u> THE WEIGHTIER MATTERS OF THE LAW, JUDGEMENT, MERCY AND FAITH: THESE YE OUGHT TO HAVE DONE, AND NOT TO LEAVE THE OTHERS UNDONE. (MATTHEW 23:23)

As we see Christ taught the Jews that they that can't half step with God. They can't do one thing and leave everything else undone. This same principle being taught applies to Marriage. Husband and wives can't think just because they're having sex with their spouse that their fulfilling their duties of Marriage. Your sex may be great, but if you're omitting honor, honesty, loyalty, etc. your love is full of hypocrisy and who desire to make love to a hypocrite? This is not to under rate the importance of Sex in a marriage because Sex is very important for the survival of a marriage, but it's not the only thing required to build a fruitful and lasting marriage. Likewise, you may be a good provider, good communicator, faithful and honest, BUT if you're not making love to your spouse those good things about you won't keep them from being tempted to step outside the marriage on you. No matter what that need needs to be met, so if you refuse to touch your spouse you are the one that's pushing them into the arms of someone that will.

TRANSFER OF POWERS

THE WIFE HATH NOT POWER OF HER OWN BODY, BUT THE HUSBAND: AND LIKEWISE ALSO THE HUSBAND HATH NOT POWER OF HIS OWN BODY BUT THE WIFE. (1 CORINTHIANS 7:2-4)

In marriage the man and the woman transfer the power of their bodies over to one another which means they no longer have power over their own bodies. This is one area where the woman has authority over her man to command his body to bow to her desires and he must surrender to her will. Whenever she wants him, he cannot close his toolbox, but instead, he must grant her access to his nuts and bolts that she may bridge the gap between them. Likewise, the woman no longer has rights over her own body, but her husband is the boss of it. He can order her to open up the highways to heaven at anytime, so that he may enter in through her pearly gates. As long as husband and wives obey this golden rule they'll never deny one another of sex. Understand, when a man or woman deny their spouse of sex they are committing sin because you can't deny your spouse of what belongs to them. Whenever your withholding it from them you are robbing them of what is rightfully theirs and anybody would get angry when you won't give them belongs to them. Husband and wives, regardless of how you may feel, when your spouse wants it, give it up!

There will be moments when couples get mad at one another and don't want to be touch each other, but as long as there isn't any irreconcilable differences, by God's law you cannot refuse one another because you have no say over your body. Even when your spouse isn't doing right by you, just think of making love to them is rendering good for their evil and stay true to upholding your part of the bargain(vow). Don't go to bed holding a grudge against one another. Lovemaking is powerful, it can be therapeutic and medicate those areas in your relationship that need healing. A couple can go all day without speaking to one another. However, they should not allow their issues to be carried into their bedroom, but allow the power of lovemaking to break down the walls of silence, bring healing, and re-open the doors of communication. In essence, regardless of how bad things get, never do your enemy's will and withhold love from each other.

If this Golden rule is kept, couples won't use their bodies as a means of manipulation as many so often do, as way of showing their spouse that their not condoning his or her behavior. Some wives practice what they call "P" control. A woman will refuse to have sex with her husband until he does something she wants him to do. Example, A woman who has become disgusted with her husband hanging out or drinking habits may resort to denying him of sex until he stops drinking and/or clubbing. However, that's not God's way of handling things. He didn't give a woman a vagina to manipulate her man with, but he gave it to her as a blessing for her husband to enjoy. She can't operate like an Indian giver and take it back from him every time she gets upset with him. Even though her husband may be out of order, she should continue to obey the Word of God and still submit to him. Likewise, the man cannot resort to "P" control. He cannot use his penis as a means of manipulation. If his wife dishonors him in any way or if she isn't acting right, he cannot punish her by withholding it from her. If anything, he need to use at as a rod of correction by giving her TOUGH LOVE in the bedroom. However, if or when a woman decides to withhold from her husband, a man cannot force her into having sex with him or that would be extortion. Extortion is a sin; therefore, no man can force or bully his wife into submission. The man cannot abuse that authority he's been given. Those who choose to retain power over their own body disobey God and hinder themselves from developing a fruitful marriage. They shall suffer the consequences of their disobedience. Husbands and wives you must give account for your own actions to God so submit to the Word and please your spouse regardless if their out of order. Through your obedience to God, your way of loving them will be better than their way of loving you and if they ever awaken to that reality, they will discover the meaning behind love never fails. Of course, if one is sick or disabled and can't function then the other must bear their cross and be patient until the other one is able. However, though your relationship might be weak in other areas, continue to light the bed with sparks. Don't let the lack of trust and communication prevent intimacy. Don't be like many married couples and use sex as a weapon against thy spouse because most couples divorce once the affection stops. Due to the lack of lovemaking they seek someone else for attention, affection, and sexual gratification.

Each one of us is held accountable for our own actions. Therefore, our primary concern should be with our own obedience and not our spouse. A man or woman should judge his or her own self daily to make sure they are in line with the Word of God and let God deal with the rebellious one. The only time married couples are **permitted** and **not commanded** to abstain from intercourse is if they both agree to abstain for a time of fasting and prayer only, but immediately after fasting has ended, it is **<u>commanded</u>** that they come together quickly, lest they be tempted for their inconsistency. The importance of consistent lovemaking in marriages is not only to keep each other's resistance strong against temptations, but SEX is a good work and God is re-warder of works; therefore, let your light shine and DO good works. Don't half-step when making love but GO ALL OUT!!! Be creative, be artistic, be exotic, and be naked and not ashamed. Making love should be a high intensive and accelerating experience every chance you get. Like DY-NO-MITE it should be explosive every time you two make contact. Don't have sex selfishly with the intent of only pleasing thyself but put in work: overtime, double time, or whatever amount of time that's required to ensure that your spouse reaches his or hers optimum level of satisfaction. If one of you is lacking in performance, practice makes it better. A wife should arise saying, "thank you Jesus" for blessing her with a man who knows how to touch and strengthen her soul and vice and versa.

If couples always abide in love, the love they share will spill over and strengthen the weak areas of their union. If they spend much time ravishing each other, they won't have time to fight one another. As their bodies touch and agree, their thoughts shall also touch and agree, their ways shall be pleasant and their souls shall dwell in peace. There is immense power in lovemaking, which is why couples should always be entangled in love. Married couples should never let a day pass or a night disappear without touching the depths of each other's soul. There is never enough love. Always and at all times, embrace and drown in each other's ocean of affection. Manage thou time right, don't let anything distract thee from doing the will of God, keep in mind making sufficient love to each other is His will. You can start forest fires, but don't start them at the same time you know you supposed to be at work, Church, or ministering to someone. Be good stewards over thy time. However, don't allow sex to interfere with taking care of The Father's Business. All the day long, in between time, lunch breaks, rest areas, always love each other. For lovemaking is the most vital part of the marriage and shall never be taken for granted. Ravish each other's bodies unceasingly. Lovemaking is one of the many pleasures and benefits of marriage. Bring thy fantasies to life, as long as a man doesn't expose his wife to another man or woman or harm her in any way, then it's alright to do what thou will in the eyes of My Lord.

For lovemaking is the exercising of the soul. The more love couples make; the stronger the marriage becomes. They're nurturing each other's soul when they touch intimately. In comparison to physical exercise, which makes you stronger, builds endurance, and flexibility. Exercising love does the same, for it's the greatest exercise couples can do to make their relationship stronger, healthier, lasting, and flexible. It becomes stronger, meaning it's harder for the enemy to pry them apart. It gets healthier, meaning they bring forth the good fruits of righteousness in their relationship. It becomes durable, meaning their relationship will last through the storm. It becomes more flexible meaning they are able to work together, being more considerate of each other's wants and needs.

When performing physical training it takes commitment and dedication to reach optimum fitness; likewise lovemaking requires the same kind of commitment and dedication to receive optimum results. Married couples should always be in the heat of passion whenever time allows because the more times you make love, It develops, defines, and tones the relationship. The stronger you make it; it strengthens and builds the marriage. Go for both repetition and strength in making love and thou art guaranteed to have great success.

When couples willfully stop making love to one another, the relationship usually comes to an end, or it cease to grow and the fruit they bore begins to wither away. It usually indicates that their desires for each other have died, and the fire of love has been quenched. The relationship weakens and digresses into misery. Therefore, to prevent the death of a marriage lovemaking should be constantly enjoyed and explored. In God's eyes sex outside marriage is a sinful act, but sex in marriage is a spiritual one. This is why Satan hates for married couples to make love, because he knows the power behind intimacy. He knows that a man gets stronger and stands firm when he makes love to the soul of his woman. For a man stands as a MAN (pounding on his chest) after he knows he has completely satisfied her soul. It reaffirms his manhood giving him the inspiration to endure the race.

For sex has been a work of God from the beginning, He made Adam and Eve ONE; He made them to be entwined in each other's locks. They were two people made one, from day one (on day six) to make love to one another. Lovemaking is putting love into action through a physical touch. It's when your bodies are having a deep and intimate conversation with one another. The essence of each other's love sends vibrations through one another's body producing an inimitable feeling.

It's a crying shame to be married and going weeks, months, and even years without touching one another. Some of these same couples use to have much sex with each other before they got married to another, but immediately after they said I DO to each other they desire ceased for one another. Isn't it odd that now, when you're married and God wants you to be thou ravished with thy spouse at all times, you find every little excuse not to be? This occurs in many marriages because those who were sexually active before marriage were gratifying the lust of their flesh and by fornication being a work of the flesh, their flesh desired sin. Once marriage took place, sex was no longer is a work of the flesh, however, sex became a deed of love, and an act of righteousness. The problem is their flesh still desires sin; their flesh will not desire their spouse because sex is no longer a sin with their spouse. Flesh desires to do evil so the only way married couple can maximize their desires for another is by renewing their mind and walking after the Spirit. Let me re emphasize that sex in marriage is a spiritual act, so you must become a spiritually minded person in-order to do what's required by God which is make love to your spouse at all times. When husband and wives are being led by the Spirit they will live joyfully together and enjoy one another in every possible way because The Spirit won't lead them any other way. However, the flesh wars against the things of the Spirit. Therefore, the flesh will never lead you to make love to your spouse, but it will automatically lead you to rebel against the command of God that tell you to be embraced in one another love at all times. The flesh will have you feeling like you don't desire your spouse at all, so in order to truly enjoy sex with thou spouse, you must renew your mind and walk after the Spirit. Your flesh must die. Carnal minded people are not subject to the law of God, so the first thing you must do is change your mind. Understand only your enemies will counsel you not to make love to another one. So when your flesh is telling you not to touch your spouse, resist your inner enemy which is indwelling sin and submit to the Spirit of God and make love to your spouse.

Sex can be a mind-blowing experience within the confines of marriage, but it is very harmful exercised outside of marriage. Fornication exposes you to immoral issues, infections, and diseases. It weakens and corrupts you, When one violates the marital vows by committing fornication they have set the grounds for divorce. That's one reason why the word commands us to flee fornication and let every man have his own wife that he/she may reap the good fruits of love.

DRINK WATERS

DRINK WATERS FROM THINE OWN CISTERN AND RUNNING
WATERS OUT OF THINE OWN WELL. ... LET THEM BE THINE
OWN AND NOT STRANGERS WITH THEE. (PROVERBS 5:15, 17)

There are many mysteries in the Gospel of Jesus Christ and
one of them is oral sex. There are married couples that still
believe that oral sex is inappropriate or that it is sin (perverse) and
that is not the truth. It's only sin when it's committed outside of
marriage. However, oral sex has been around since the beginning
of time. As we search the scriptures in the book of Proverbs, My
Lord commands a man to drink water from his own cistern. A
cistern is the Hebrew word "bowr", which means a pit hole, well,
fountain or dungeon. There are two ways to drink water physically
and spiritually. As spiritual people, our bodies are referenced
occasionally as cisterns and wells and out of our bellies shall flow
rivers of living water. Everything we need rests inside of us. God
has blessed us with an abundance of resources. As long as we walk
according to His Word there shall be an overflow of love, joy,
peace, goodness, gentleness, faith, temperance, meekness,
longsuffering abiding in our spirit because The Spirit of God will
literally dwells in us as a river fall of living waters. In Proverbs
when a man is instructed to drink water from his own cistern, he is
being instructed to drink only from his wife. In other words, his
woman should be a well full of wealth (water). The Word of God
abiding in her that is rich in mercy should be able to supply her
man with the strength, encouragement, comfort, and support he
needs. She should have an unlimited supply of water that her
man can draw from her at any given time quenching the thirst of
his soul. There should never be a need for him to look to another
woman to give him anything.

From a physical aspect, a Christian woman should be a well
that never runs dry. She should be a very passionate woman

127

desiring her husband always. Her water should be pure and sweet to his soul. Likewise, the woman should drink of her man. She should be well drunken from the strength of his love. The love couples have for one another should be an unquenchable flame of fire, "HOT" at all times and their passion should never die. Husbands and wives should never hesitate to draw and taste of one another. For Solomon knew the power behind drinking water and what it can do to a woman.

AND THE ROOF OF THY MOUTH LIKE THE BEST OF WINE FOR MY BELOVED, THAT GOETH DOWN SWEETLY CAUSING THE LIPS OF THOSE THAT ARE ASLEEP TO SPEAK. I AM MY BELOVED AND HIS DESIRE IS TOWARD ME. (SONG OF SONGS 7: 9)

Solomon and his woman undoubtedly got busy. Solomon knew how to awaken his woman out of sleep and get her undivided attention. For in the scripture, she describes how sweet his mouth is to her as it journeys down her body, like wine traveling down her soul. For it stimulated her mind and aroused every emotion in her body, and quickened her from a state of unconsciousness. When he drunk of her water it made her body quiver. It made her speak with confidence of who she was to him and gave her confirmation of his desires for her. He brought her joy and she felt it in her soul. She knew that her man loved to be in the corridors of her courts. He referred to her body as a secret garden and he delighted in every inch of her.

A GARDEN INCLOSED IS MY SISTER, MY SPOUSE; A SPRING SHUT UP, A FOUNTAIN SEALED. THY PLANTS ARE AN ORCHARD OF POMEGRANETS, WITH PLEASANT FRUITS; CAMPHIRE, WITH SPIKENARD, SPIKENARD AND SAFFRON; CALAMUS AND CINNAMON, WITH ALL TREES OF FRANKINCENSE; MYRRY AND ALOES, WITH ALL CHIEF SPICES; A FOUNTAIN OF GARDENS, A WELL OF LIVING WATERS, AND STREAMS FROM LEBANON. AWAKE, O NORTH WIND; AND COME, THOU SOUTH; BLOW UPON MY GARDEN THAT THE SPICES THEREOF MAY FLOW OUT. LET MY BELOVED COME INTO HIS GARDEN; AND EAT HIS PLEASANT FRUITS. (SONG OF SONGS 4: 12-16)

There is great peace in knowing that your spouse desires you. To know that you are in their mind, and that you have what it takes to turn them on and to completely satisfy them, makes you more confident of your relationship and brings gladness to the heart. Look at the passage above how Solomon's wife invites him to come into her. She describes her body as garden full of fruits and desire for him to come and eat of the pleasant fruits of her body. A woman's genital area is one of the fruits of the body. She went as far as summoning the winds to help prepare the way for her beloved. The winds blew softly upon her fruits and sent an irresistible scent into the air. Her aroma filled the atmosphere, for it was the flow of her spices that ushered him into complete ecstasy with her. She didn't have any unsavory odors. Her body, her private parts, her essence smelled good! A natural irresistible scent that drew him to her vineyard that he may taste of her fruits and drink of her waters. He acknowledged streams flowed from her.

Husbands and wives need to spice it up and they should never be afraid to touch one another intimately. A man should never make his wife feel uneasy, if she wants to make love to him in different ways and vice versa. Some people make their spouse feel bad because they might have a high sex drive and/or he or she might want to drink water and there is nothing wrong with it. It's to be shared between two people that have become one body. There isn't any stronger display of love in a marriage than lovemaking. The day you stop making love to your spouse is the day he or she will ask, "Is it that you don't love me anymore?" "Are you not attracted to me?" To prevent your spouse from thinking that there's anything wrong, you need to show yourself faithful in that department. Lovemaking is the greatest way to connect. You can commune over the phone, through Internet, letters, via satellite, but when you come face-to-face and express your desires for one another through "ORAL" communication it's illuminating. Oral sex is nothing to be ashamed of. When a man drinks water from his woman he is reassuring her that he desires her. The feeling it produces is so intense that it brings her out of sleep and energizes her to endure the night of vehement passion. Every part of her that was tired, lazy, and sleepy will strengthened from the stroke of his tongue. When a man's lips kiss her in that spot it raises her body temperature and makes her want to shout. There wouldn't be anything she wouldn't want to do. If she didn't feel like making love before he got went there, she won't be able to stop from wanting make love after his lips have taken a journey to her vine.

Couples that don't practice it have their right not to, but that option is always available if they chose too. Many turn their nose up at it, many think it is perverse, however, there shouldn't be any part of lovemaking left uncharted. Oral sex has its benefits and it takes you to another dimension of intimacy producing more love and happiness in the bedroom. There is nothing disgraceful or shameful about it when done in marriage. Homosexuals have taken this act and perverted it which also proves that oral sex outside is a sin. That's the main reason why God destroyed Sodom and Gomorrah, however, that also proves that oral sex has been around since the beginning of time. In marriage your body belongs to your spouse; therefore, don't deny thy spouse access to drink. When God created Adam and Eve he didn't give them restrictions on how to make love and multiply. The law didn't come till Moses and there is no place in the law that forbids drinking water from your spouse.

Why would you feel it's disgusting to eat fruit or drink water from your husband and/or wife? Water is good and refreshes a thirsty soul. Therefore, husbands and wives should drink from each other whenever they get hot and thirsty. Example, when runners in a marathon become overheated, they will drink water to rejuvenate themselves, it gives them more strength to continue their race. Likewise, drinking water from your spouse works accordingly in love making. When your spouse is tired and thinks that he or she can't go any longer, take a water break and notice how quickly a surge of energy arises in them.

Eating Fruits and Drinking Waters enriches the relationship and enhances sexual escapades. It's also a way for a woman to please her man while she's on her menstruation, or during her 6 week healing process after she has given birth, or any other physical ailment that could prevent her from intercourse. Likewise, this is a way a husband can please his woman, that's if he's impotent. Also many people are afflicted with incurable diseases such as Herpes, HPV (venereal warts). Though man can't cure these diseases all things are possible with God, for there is nothing he can't cure, if you just believe. However, some of these diseases afflict people with reoccurring breakouts and during the time of the blisters, warts, or sores appearing, they are not suppose to have sex because it's highly contagious at that time. Let's assume that a man has herpes and his wife does not, whenever he has a breakout, he shouldn't have sex with he, but he can eat of her fruits to satisfy her soul. This works both ways unless a person's mouth is infected and in that case couples must be patient and wait until the coast is clear.

Some disagree with this understanding of the scripture of Drinking Waters, in that it has a sexual orientation. For those who disagree then consider the scripture below.

WHOSO IS SIMPLE, LET HIM TURN HITHER: AND AS FOR HIM THAT WANTETH UNDERSTANDING SHE SAITH TO HIM, <u>STOLEN WATERS ARE SWEET</u>, AND BREAD EATEN IN SECRET IS PLEASANT. BUT HE KNOWETH NOT THAT THE DEAD ARE THERE, AND HER GUEST IS IN THE DEPTHS OF HELL. (PROVERBS 9:16, 17)

What does the adulteress woman mean when she is enticing a man to sin by saying stolen waters are sweet? What is she referring to when she said bread eaten in secret is pleasant? She is obviously referring to a secret sexual relationship. In this passage, a married woman is seducing a man to sleep with her and whenever a man covets another man's wife, he desires to draw water from a well that doesn't belong to him. Thus, whenever thou lay with a married person thou art stealing water and eating the bread of deceit. It might seem all good, but he that commits adultery with a woman destroys his own soul. Many men are not only in hell, but they are in the lowest hell, jail, sickbed, tormented, etc. on earth because they slept or is having an affair with a foolish married woman. Men void of understanding are driven by lust and fall into many snares and traps such as this.

Husbands and wives be true to one another and be thankful that God has given you the right to explore all avenues of lovemaking without fear. You never have to fear that you are displeasing God when you are exploring different methods of pleasing one another sexually. That's one of the reasons why God ordained marriage that you may enjoy one another freely. Some women and men might have a big problem with drinking water from their spouse. Either they don't like it or they think it's disgusting. Remember, love is not selfish meaning though you might not care to do certain things, you can't think about yourself. Lovemaking is not one sided, if it makes your spouse happy and as long as it is not against or distracting you from the will of God, then why not please your spouse. Seek to satisfy one another in every way. Therefore, you're not leaving any room for the enemy to get his foot in it. In conclusion, don't do anything you don't have peace with. Pray about all things, wait on God to give you peace and proceed without fear.

PREHEAT THE OVEN

And because iniquity shall abound, the love of many shall wax cold.
(Matthew 24:1)

Some couples started off hot, heated, and heavy from the first time they laid eyes on each other, but over time they began to lose desires for one another. Sin infected their relationship causing their love for each other to wax cold, thus, their relationship is frozen. Cold means having little or no warmth: lacking in passion, emotion, enthusiasm, not affectionate, cordial, or friendly, unresponsive, depressing, dispiriting, faint, and weak. These are all warnings that your relationship is below temperature. You feel you can't talk to that person, so there's little or no communication. You have become numb to everything that person says or does. You challenge one another constantly and you do your best to try to stay out of each other's way. You behave rudely and cruel towards one another. You're not happy at all and the worse part about it is, although you abide together you still feel all alone. You stand against one another more than you do in support of each other so, the sex has become ice cold. It doesn't necessarily mean that sex has altogether ceased but does imply that sex has become less frequent, robotic and with no umph in it. It has become like trying to cook something without preheating the oven and what's the point of sticking raw meat on a cold grill? In relations to sex FOREPLAY is like preheating her oven and once the oven is hot, then at that time and not a moment before, is when you should stick the meat in it, so it can start cooking immediately. Foreplay is an essential part of lovemaking because it grants you the opportunity to search out and learn your partner's body and discover different ways for a man to heat up her oven and for her to defrost his meat. Understand before the main event there's always an opening act to prepare you mentally and/or physically for the primary episode. Examples, there's stretching before exercising, a prelude before the premiere attraction, there's appetizers before the entree, and sometimes the appetizers can be so good and fulfilling to you, that you may be too full to eat the entree. Foreplay is the intro to lovemaking. It includes the kissing, the caressing, the fondling, the oral, any or everything that stimulates the mind and the body leading up to the actual act of penetration. Foreplay when done thoroughly can cause both of you to reach maximum orgasms without ever sticking meat on the oven.

Again, in the beginning of any relationship the DESIRE for one another is strong, you usually can't keep your hands off another, but to maintain those strong desires what you speak is very important. Wives your mouth is the thermostat that controls →the temperatures← of your Man. The words you speak can affect his bedroom performance, it can either stimulate his desires for you or cause him to lose all desires for you. If you're speaking harsh bitter words against him, if you're talking to him in a disrespectful tone, if you're murmuring and complaining, etc. those things can quench his thirst for you. Likewise husbands the same rule applies with you, a woman can lose the desire to defrost your meat, if you're talking to her sideways. You can't cut her with words and then expect her to have any desire to jump your bones. Clear signs that your desires are fading away is when the preheating stops. You won't desire to kiss, cuddle, caress, or freak on another. Whenever you have sex it won't feel like you're making love it will become a dry, robotic, forced action and instead of seeking to gratify each other's soul, you're just trying to get one off. This should not be the case.

It's not too late to change things around, but both of you must be willing to make all the necessary steps to raise your relationship out of freezing temperature. First step is to be **HONEST** with one another. You must admit all your mistakes because you can't repair anything if you don't even acknowledge your part in breaking it. Second step is **FORGIVENESS**. If you truly want your relationship to work, you must forgive one another from the heart for all the things you've done wrong to each other. Forgiving them does not mean you trust them because maybe their actions exposed they can't be trusted. However, forgiveness removes the hurt that their actions caused you and allows you to freely love them without holding anything against them. The Third step is **PRAYER**. After you've reconciled and forgiven one another because you can't go before God angry with each other then you need to pray for one another. When you're praying for another it's like performing CPR on a marriage that has stop breathing. Prayer is a critical part of the recovery process because in order for relationship to live, you need divine intervention. You need the power of God to breathe life back into it because if He doesn't do it, it cannot be done. **LOVE** is the anecdote and if you are afraid to love them, you will never produce the heat needed to survive, thus, your only wasting your time. However, the more you LOVE one another in deed and in truth you won't focus on each other mistakes. You will think about all the reasons you need to hold on instead of the reasons you need to let go. When you love one another all the good things you do for one another will bury all the wrong that's been done. Last thing is **PATIENCE**. Understand it takes time for things to heal, so don't expect things to change immediately, but if you hold on to Gods unchanging hand, in time He'll mend all those broken pieces back together again. In conclusion, above all things LOVE one another and remember and would be wise of you to preheat the oven before sticking on the grill understanding that

Hatred stirreth up strifes: but LOVE covereth all sins.(Proverbs 10:12)

BEDROOM HEAT

Again, if two lie together, then they have heat: but how can one be warm alone? (Ecclesiastes 4:11)

One of the beauties of Marriage is that you have the answer to COLD NIGHTS laying right beside you. When the temperatures drop and your joints become stiff, you never have to touch the thermostat, put on extra clothing, nor turn on an electric heater, all you have to do is roll over because your spouse can provide you with all the heat you need. He or she needs to be your cup of hot coffee because the affection and love needed to warm you, can be generated when you make good use of their body, which God blessed you to have power over. Understand there is no better way to create heat than lovemaking and the stronger you make it the greater the heat. So, instead of lying at the corners of the bed complaining about the weather and refusing to touch each other, let your bodies communicate with each other during those dark and cold nights because FRICTION is the best natural WAY to increase BODY temperature. Draw nigh to God through prayer, draw nigh to one another in heart, and draw nigh to one another in body and make love without ceasing. Your bedroom should be as a burning furnace and the way you love one another should cause your bed to turn into a wild blazing fire and not a small brush of smoke. If you do not love each other the right way your touch shall be as cold waters putting out the flames.

Lovemaking should be intense and dimensional; for it's a verb (action word). Therefore, it should always be in motion going to the next level of glory. It should be an audible moment of ecstasy. The resonance of your voices when love is being made should penetrate through the walls. For when a man embraces the bosom of his woman it complements her soul. Where there is an argument, strife, discord, or disagreement, the implementation of lovemaking can conquer all of that. For love covers all sins. For lovemaking is a bedroom odyssey having more than a thousand and one ways to travel.

Some are not creating bedroom heat because they no longer desire their spouses physically, being that their spouses made the big mistake of letting their physical appearance crumble right after saying I DO. Husband and wives you can't stop caring about yourself when you get married because your body is not your own. If five years into the marriage and you're fifty plus pounds smaller or bigger, refusing to work out and/or eat right , not taking good care of you hygiene and wondering why your spouse is not in the mood, maybe it's because you let yourself go. If you love your spouse, love is not selfish; therefore, if you can't get it together for yourself, get it together for your spouse. When you get married it's not just about you any longer because as the word of God teaches us, you hath not power over your own body but your spouse does, so keep it together for him or her. Men if you was working out before you got married, don't willfully stop working out after you get married, wives if you kept it sexy before you had children, keep it sexy after you have children. You can't lose everything that was physically desirable to your spouse and expect for their desires for you to be the same. Do what you have to do to maintain the fire in the bedroom. Although that's not an excuse for a husband or wife to cheat on each other, the reality is that issue has driven many men and women into secret love affairs. Your physical appearance doesn't define who you are nor does it produce any results; so your beauty doesn't mean you will have a fruitful marriage. However, understand sex and affection are physical acts, so maintain your appearance because it can be hard for your spouse to perform those acts with you if they cease from being physically attracted to you. Especially if your appearance was the only or the main thing they desired about you. This is why you shouldn't marry someone who you know that solely wants to marry you because of their physical attraction towards you. Surely their desire for you will fade the day your beauty fades. This is one of the reasons why husbands and wives must be considerate of one another and try their best not to lose those things that are appealing to one another. It's one thing when nature takes its course or when a storm comes in your life and corrupts your beauty because those are out of your control and in such cases, husbands and wives should be very patient, understanding, compassionate, and endure the storm with one another, but it's another thing to get married and let yourself go because in that case you're doing it to yourself. You are your worst enemy being found guilty of being inconsiderate and careless. When you're married it's not just about you anymore. Your spouse should be an incentive for you to keep yourself looking appetizing. You should want to look in their eyes.

In conclusion, don't stop caring about how you look, smell, talk, act etc. because those are some of the very same reasons why your spouse fell in love you and just as a person fell in love with you, they can fall out of love with you also. If you want your relationship to change for the better, you must always aim to change for the better. You can't take a turn for the worse after you get married by stopping the romance, the surprises, fitness, work ethic, cleanliness, and everything you did that made them desire and want to marry you. The things you do for another shouldn't decrease in marriage but increase. Everything should continually get better, so don't let the fire of your love simmer but do those things required of you that turns up the heat. You can't stop putting logs in the fire and get mad when you find yourself without heat.

LET HER BE

LET HER BE AS A LOVING HIND AND A PLEASANT ROE LET HER BREAST SATISFY THEE AT ALL TIMES; AND BE THOU RAVISHED ALWAYS WITH HER LOVE AND WHY WILT THOU, MY SON, BE RAVISHED WITH A STRANGE WOMAN, AND EMBRACE THE BOSOM OF A STRANGER? (PROVERBS 5:19)

Too many men are having affairs on their wives but men, why would you step outside of your wife to get what you can get from YOUR WIFE? Why would you go to a strip club and pay for whorish women to do things that your wife can do for you in the privacy of your own home? Why roam the streets in search of easy sleazy women to sleep with you and take the chance of bringing venereal diseases back home with you? A strange woman is any woman outside of your wife because those women are not the woman you vowed to love. Stop seeking to get your freak on with females that don't belong to you. The woman you need is at home and able to perform everything those other strange women are doing for you.

There are many things women would love to do for their man, but out of fear of being judged by their man, many of them suppress their desires. They don't say some of the sexual things they want to say or do many of the explicit things they desire to do because they don't want their man to look at them in a negative way. Brothers, don't utter things to your woman that would cause her to bury the passion she has in her. This is the reason God commands a man not to prohibit his woman from being that loving hind and a pleasant roe and to LET HER BE. Never imply or make her feel like she's a whorish woman simply because she desire to explore and do sexually explicit things with you. Don't make her feel abnormal because her body always craves too feel you inside of her. As her man stay intoxicated with her love. LET her be as freaky as she want to be and bring to reality all the desires of her mind that falls within the realms of God. You can have anal sex, oral sex, vaginal sex, freaky sex, hot and steamy sex, etc. As long as she is with you and you ALONE, you can have any kind of sex you want to. Brother, don't dare try to make her feel that it's not of God for her to always want to feel YOU inside of her. She needs to be your massage therapist, your physical therapist, your exotic dancer, your hot chocolate, your naked chef, your personal porn star, etc. Allow her to be those things with you, so she won't be tempted to be those things with someone else, that would love for her to be those things that you didn't her to be for you.

AT ALL TIMES

There is never a wrong time for a man to make love to his woman. My Lord commands a man to AT ALL TIMES let her breast satisfy him and to always be ravished with her love. If every man obeyed those instructions, there wouldn't be any woman complaining about the lack of affection they're getting from their husband. Understand husbands, God wants you to make love to your spouse; he wants you to enjoy HER, so give her deep and passionate love. Wives don't get upset if your man wants sex from you all the time, but rather acknowledge and commend his obedience to the Word of God and satisfy his craving for you. Men don't make your wife feel like it's ungodly of her to desire you all the time, but rather understand that she was made for you. It would be strange if she did not desire you. If she didn't want to feel you inside of her that's when you need to be concerned. There should never be dull moments in your marriage. Husband and wives shouldn't lay at the edge of the bed refusing to make love to one another. If you're not in the mood, deny yourself and "make love" any way and surely once you heat the room, it will change the mood. If you're mad "make love" and surely that will calm your anger, that kind of love making is called Sexual healing. A child of God has the image and likeness of God. Any man who does not love his wife according to the Word of God is not walking in the image of God. A righteous man must do right to his woman and vice verse!

MAKE LOVE TO HER

Men if you have a problem with touching your wife. Then the question is WHY? Because the last thing that a women should ever have to be concerned about or complain about is you not touching her. If she didn't do anything that quenched your desire, yet you have no desire, then of course it would provoke to question your faithfulness and/or sexuality. In her mind, either our cheating or you gay. If she tells any of her friends about you the first thing they will shout is that you are gay. The man's body was uniquely designed with specific accessories that enables him to become one with his wife. It grants him to power to enter her, so that she can feel the strength of his manhood which is able to take to her to the seventh heaven. Therefore, don't think just because your woman desires for you to transport her to the state of euphoria at all times that she's an out of control nymphomaniac. If she loves how you make her feel, then its normal for her to want to feel you. Don't quench her desire for you by making foolish comments such as, "You just like that rest of these hoes." Don't insult her just because she wants to get freaky with you. Comments such as those will only suppress her desires for you and cause her to withdraw from you. So as her man, you need to awaken every erotic emotion in her body and let her be one that bring all your fantasies to life. Don't let days pass by without making love to her, whatever you do don't deny her of you and vice versa.

DEFRAUD YE NOT ONE ANOTHER, EXCEPT IT BE WITH CONSENT FOR A TIME, THAT YE MAY GIVE YOURSELVES TO FASTING AND PRAYER, AND COME TOGETHER AGAIN, THAT SATAN TEMPT YOU NOT FOR YOUR INCONTINENCY. (1 CORINTHIANS 7:5)

A man should allow his wife to be what she was specifically designed to be, and not make her feel uncomfortable because she desires to be his everything. Why would any man want to provoke his woman to find affection elsewhere? If he lets her be as the loving hind, she shouldn't have a desire to be elsewhere. When she desires to feed thee breakfast in bed and to be thou breakfast in bed, let her be. For when she desires to be thy dessert and the icing on your cake, let her be. Don't hesitate to embrace her because your hands should be full of her. There are parts of her, you should **never** stop touching and there is no part of you, you should restrict her from touching. Let her be a bundle of love and deny her not of her rights to be your wife. Through still and troubled waters you should love her, and let the Christ in her be the strength you need when you wax weak. Let her be the ear that listens when you need someone to talk to. Let her be the body that produces the heat you need on cold nights. Let her be the hands that massage every part of you that's needs a loving touch. Let her be the friend that sticks closer than a brother. Let her be the mother of your children. Let the Christ in her provide you the peace you need in stressful times and also Let the Christ in her be the well of living waters that you draw from when thirsty. She should be a comfort to thee in good and bad times. If thou let her be, she should be a joy in the midst of sorrow having the radiance of the sun brightening all your cloudy days. She should be as a full moon in the darkest night giving you light. Let her be your eye's desire, let her be the lover of your soul. When a man lets his woman be, it will be a blessing to him, his days shall be enriched with goodness and mercy and his life full of joy. For a man will never experience the fullness of happiness in his marriage until he let his wife be. Don't restrain, withhold, or resist her love, but consume her love by Letting Her Be!

BED OF INTEGRITY

**MARRIAGE IS HONOURABLE IN ALL AND THE BED UNDEFILED.
(HEBREWS 13:14)**

Marriage is an exclusive relationship between a man and his woman that has been sealed by the Creator. It is as if God has given a man and his woman a license to have sex exclusively with one another. Those who are having sex without the license are in violation of God's law and their bed is defiled meaning unclean. Different cultures have different ways to marry. However, rather your marriage was arranged or you chose your spouse, all marriages are to be respected and those who disrespect a marriage has disrespected the Law of God.

Marriage is a lifetime commitment of loyalty you make before God to love, honor, respect, and abide with the one your soul should love. Why get married if you know you don't have any intentions on being true it? Why stay married if you're not honoring the commitment you made? And what's the point of getting married if you're "sharing" your spouse? Yet, this is case with them that have corrupted the beauty of their marriage. They have no fear of God and turned their holy matrimony into a freak show. Instead of being his wife she has become her husband's whore. Instead of being her husband he has become her pimp. Instead of keeping strangers out their bed, they've turned their mattress into a host for threesomes, a bed for swingers, and a lodge for orgies. Everything that supposes to be sacred in their marriage they' made it sinister. This should not be the case, husbands and wives should be each other's personal "freak," and their sexual activities should be a private love affair and not a world's exhibition.

Don't allow the serpent to seduce you to eat forbidden fruit which is what swingers would call the Lifestyle. The Lifestyle is a spruced of up way of saying your living a lifestyle of whoredom. Although the pleasures of the sin may be great, the end result of those things is death. Don't wait until the pain outweighs the pleasure before you try to stop. If that's the lifestyle your living, repent now and understand that in marriage your bed is purified; sex is a clean and lawful in the eyes of My Lord. He has not put any restraints on married couples; they are commanded to enjoy one another fully. Romance and lovemaking should be in motion at all times. The sex is un-prohibited and couples are encouraged to have it as often as they like. Their bed is undefiled as long as it's a private party. If a man or woman brings outsiders into their bedroom, they transform their bed into an abomination.

A man should not expose his wife's body to anyone else. He supposes to be the only one to till her ground, water her plants and eat of her fruits. He shouldn't turn what suppose to be a private and sacred garden to him into a public zoo. However, this has been the case with many couples who have lusted exceedingly, so God gave them up to the lust of their own heart in order to commit those vile affection

WHEREFORE GOD ALSO GAVE THEM UP TO THE UNCLEANNESS THROUGH THE LUSTS OF THEIR OWN HEARTS, TO DISHONOUR THEIR OWN BODIES BETWEEN THEMSELVES... FOR THIS CAUSE GOD GAVE THEM UP TO VILE AFFECTIONS; FOR EVEN THEIR WOMEN DID CHANGE THE NATURAL USE INTO THAT WHICH WAS AGAINST NATURE: AND LIKEWISE ALSO THE MEN LEAVING THE NATURAL USE OF A WOMAN, BURNED IN THEIR LUST ONE TOWARD ANOTHER; MEN WITH MEN WORKING THAT WHICH IS UNSEEMLY, AND RECEIVING IN THEMSELVESS THAT RECOMPENSE OF THEIR ERROR WHICH WAS MEET. AND EVEN AS THEY DID NOT LIKE TO RETAIN GOD IN THEIR KNOWLEDGE, GOD GAVE THEM OVER TO A REPROBATE MIND, TO DO THOSE THINGS WHICH ARE NOT CONVENIENT...WHO KNOWING THAT THEY WHICH DO SUCH THINGS ARE WORTHY OF DEATH, NOT ONLY DO THE SAME, BUT HAVE PLEASURE IN THEM THAT DO THEM. (ROMANS 1:23-28, 32)

Marriage is a heavenly design. It's not something man

conjured up, but it's a work of God and Satan hates it. He doesn't want a man to enjoy a woman physically, mentally, and spiritually free from sin. The thought of a man making love to a woman without have fear of catching a disease, or producing an ungodly seed torments his mind. He desires for us to fall into sexual sins because it's a trap of death. Though we are commanded to repent from all sin, notice that fornication is the only sin in the Gospel that it emphasizes to flee from. Fornication is the only sin committed against the body, meaning you offend and dishonor your own body, which is the Lord's temple. So respect his body and repent from all uncleanness. Most sicknesses and diseases are transmitted through fornications. Therefore, people who practice fornications put themselves in great risk of getting afflicted.

My Lord expect for a man and his wife to maintain bedroom integrity, if he does that, he will never allow strangers into his room nor will he lead his woman into swingers clubs, strip-joints, freak parties, or influence her to participate in three-sums, bestiality, homosexuality, etc. He won't encourage her to do drugs, drink alcohol, behave foolish or vile in anyway. He won't lead her into doing anything displeasing to Christ. A woman of integrity would get offended by her husband asking her to do certain things such as that with him. It would be an insult to her character. She would ask you, What type of woman do you think she is? Or what type of woman are you trying to TURN her into? Her being the type of woman she is would never suggest those things to her man. She understands as a wife the importance of submitting to her husband but she know by no means does the Lord require her to become a fool for her husband.

Wives if you're a-->woman of Integrity<--or if you're trying to become one, it should be an insult to your character for your man to even suggest sharing you with another woman or man. If he wants to share you with another man, he's basically saying you're a whore, and if he wants to share you with another woman, if you're not bisexual, he's trying to lead you into homosexuality and calling you a whore. What "MAN" gets turned on by seeing TWO women together? Surely he isn't a Man of God! And what Man gets turned on by seeing another Man with his woman. Open your eyes sister, men who suggest that to you don't give a crap about you, their just looking for an unreserved whore they can use and satisfy their foolish lust upon. Don't allow men to pass your vagina around like a collection plate.

Brothers if you are a--->Man of integrity<-- cultivate the woman and lead her down paths of righteousness, don't drive them into darkness. Our Sisters need us strong. We can't expect them to do right when we are all wrong! The thought of having multiple woman in bed at one time may be very tempting and the pleasure may be great, but the disgrace & shame it causes you is far greater than any pleasure it brings you. So, don't allow whorish women to seduce you into a pool of sin and a world of hurt. Many brothers have lost their family and betrayed good women for whorish ones who brought them low. Many men are infected right now because they lacked the self control to not place their pipe into anything that has a hole in it. A man or woman of integrity" won't influence you to do things that cause you to lay aside your integrity; If it takes more than you in the bedroom to please them YOU NEED to leave them.

Proverbs 11:3 The integrity of the upright shall guide them: but the perverseness of transgressors shall destroy them.

If you build your marriage THE WAY God designed it to be, it will be a beautiful monogamous loving relationship. They have exclusive rights to enjoy each other's bodies. However, many have redefined God's definition of Marriage. They have corrupted the sanctity and holiness of their marital bed by sharing it with STRANGERS! Some wives have foolishly brought in other women into their bedroom to either fulfill their husbands fantasies of having multiple women at one time. Although, they are doing it to please their husbands, in many cases it results in them losing all respect for their wives. Some women bring other women into their bedroom to gratify their own same sex attraction and men that allow them to, often end up losing their spouse to the gay community. Men who influence their wives into the "Life-Style," which is when married couples swap spouses, engage in orgies, freak parties and have sex with others in front of each other. Some of them have certain guidelines they follow, such as they can't have sex with anyone else if they're not present. However, if your man or woman is willing to have sex while you're there. It would be unwise of you to believe he or she wouldn't have sex when you're not around. Secondly, there are many disease ridden HIV positive people that are intentionally going these Life-Style events trying to infect as many people as they can, so what type of" LIFESTYLE" do you think they live? Wouldn't swingers parties & freak clubs be the perfect places for them to attend? If you care about your life and marriage you won't share your spouse and expose to him or her to that nonsense! What kind of sick man are you to find pleasure in seeing another man or woman climb in your wife? What kind of sick woman are you getting excited seeing your husband dig into another woman or man? The Life-Style is not something new under the sun, but it's spreading faster than aids. It's becoming an acceptable behavior amongst many couples that has obviously come to the conclusion that monogamy isn't gratifying enough, so they have decided to spice up their marriage by turning their BED of INTEGRITY into a BED of WHOREDOMS, but they shall face the JUDGMENT OF GOD!

CHAPTER SIX

LOVE HER SO

6

LOVE HER SO

HUSBANDS LOVE YOUR WIVES, EVEN AS CHRIST ALSO LOVED THE CHURCH, AND GAVE HIMSELF FOR IT. THAT HE MIGHT PRESENT IT TO HIMSELF A GLORIOUS CHURCH, NOT HAVING SPOT OR WRINKLE OR ANY SUCH THING: BUT THAT IT BE HOLY AND WITHOUT BLEMISH. (EPHESIANS 5: 25-27)

My Lord made it a law for a man to love his woman **(Wife)** as much as He loved His Church, that means to love her so much that he will become her eyes when she can't see, her ears when she can't hear, her legs when she can't walk, her voice when she can't speak, and her hands when she can't hold on. Be her strength when she waxes weak and her pillow when she needs to lay her head. Be her cappuccino in the morning and be as cold waters to her thirsty soul and let her drink of thee all the day. Let her sip you and then let her swallow you. Let her taste every bit of you. When she gets confused help her make her decisions. Be as a father when she needs to feel secure and that strength of you putting your foot down. Foremost, be her lord and together worship The Lord. Give her thy soul and love her so. Love her to the point people will not believe it's possible to love someone that much. Love her so much that it lasts through every trial, temptation, and test. Everything that your enemies do to tempt you to leave her, should only make you love her more. Many shall say you've lost your mind for loving her so strongly, but that's not true, you only love the way My Lord has commanded thee to.

A woman has depths and her man should touch her softly in those deep places. He should always be caught up in the rapture of her love. Do not love her the way many women have been taught to love a man. Many are taught not to love a man **until** he gets his own house, car, money, etc. Therefore, they only love you **until** you lose your house, car, money etc. Satan always gives them an excuse on why not to love a man. Therefore, be the opposite and love her **Now**. Don't wait until she gets her act together, loses weight, make a lot of money, buys a car or house, etc. Love her anyway and help her get there. Love her while she's in the process, not after she's complete, because those who didn't know her or want her before will want to love her **Then**. Therefore, love her **Now** before **Then** and love her **Now** before **Them**. For their love isn't real. Be her first and her last. Love her beginning and her end. Love her **Now** and **Then**. Love her so and let her know that she needs nothing, but **JESUS!** Love her so much that time doesn't tick long enough to show her how deep your feelings are. Love her so that other women regardless of how fine they are, or how much money they have, will not move you or even give you the slightest thought to betray her. At all costs, bear your cross and love her so. If you must die to save her, then lay down thy life. Become the man that she needs you to become. Deny thyself, stop drinking, smoking, cursing, being whorish, forsake the foolish, and fear My Lord. Become strong and wrestle against thine enemies. Be Satan's nightmare and fight for thy woman.

My Lord so loved His Church (Lamb's bride) that he suffered, was crucified, and went to hell to save and sanctify it. He's longsuffering and very merciful to us while we are stubborn and rebellious. However, he knew we were lost and that our minds were darkened; therefore, He paid the price that he might bring us into His marvelous light. He bore His cross and overcame the enemy. Many rose up against Him with incensed hatred, lying, and falsely accusing Him of every sinful act in the book, even now they call Him a deceiver, but everything they put Him through was purposed. They put Him through hell, but He was stronger than hell. They thought by nailing Him to a cross, He would give up, but that was the purpose of His manifestation. He went to hell for three days and three nights for His bride. That's too much love and My Lord commands a man to love his woman so much that he would do the same for her as Jesus did for His Church.

Once the Church realizes what My Lord did for her, how He suffered, fought, and died for her, the Church is and will be sick in love with Him as Solomon's wife was sick in love with him, but it will be a greater love than that. To be sick in love is to love someone so much that you get butterflies in your stomach every time you think of them, all you can do is wonder, think, and yearn to be with them. They're in your mind, heart, and in your spirit. You love them so much you will do **anything** to please them. You'll find pleasure in pleasing them. You're in love to the point that it's sickening to other people. Friends and family will call you a fool for him/her because you're willing to do whatever is required to be with him or her. If you must forsake family, close your door on some friends, relocate, etc. you will pay the cost.

When a man loves his woman the way My Lord loves His Church, if her eyes are not opened and she's taken that love for granted, once they do open, expect to be most blessed by her. She shall love her man so much that it makes her people sick. They will get tired of her talking about him. They will be jealous of her relationship with him. She will be past the point of wanting to be with him. She will feel a void when he's not there. It will be her soul that loves him. She won't want to carry on without him. Every time he departs from her presence, she will be anxiously waiting on him to come back, as the Church is waiting on My Lord to come back. She will want her man all the day, and all through the night. It won't matter what she has to go through to be with him, as long as she is with him.

When you find the one whom your soul loveth, the first thing devil try to do is get into your mind by berating or degrading that person to you, they'll give you a thousand and one reasons why you shouldn't desire that person. If that person is godly, he or she will be persecuted. The world must hate, lie, and condemn him or her. Therefore, prepare your heart to fight the devil. Don't let persecution cause you to fall away from someone that could be the biggest blessing to your soul. Satan will go as far to pay you not to become involved with certain godly people. For that is how much he hates them and he hates to see you with him/her because he knows your relationship with him will no longer be.

The devil will do whatever he can to stop you from being with the one whom My Lord predestined you to become one with. He often tries to creep into the woman's mind first since she is the weaker vessel, therefore, a man should love his woman so much that if she gets lost, he will fervently pray that My Lord restores her soul. Ask My Lord to open her eyes before it is too late and until time runs out, love her soul by loving her so.

SO LOVE HER

The love of a man should be so deep for his woman that it has no boundaries. Love her for who she is and love her more for who she will become in Christ. Love all of her. Love her eyes, Love her ears, Love her lips, Love her body, Love her Spirit and Love her Soul. You Love her eyes by allowing her to SEE your love and put nothing wicked before them, gaze deep into them and look into her soul. You love her lips by kissing them constantly and feed them delicious and sweet fruits. Listen to her as she speaks. You love her ears by speaking the truth and words of life into them. You love her heart by securing it safely, so that she can walk with the confidence of knowing that you are there for her. Render acts of kindness that bless her heart with peace and joy. You Love her Spirit by edifying it with the Word and exercising godliness with her. You Love her body by making love to it without ceasing. Handle it with care without ever physically abuse her or encouraging her to do anything that could be harmful to her body. You love her soul by leading her down paths righteousness and touching her in deep places. No part of her can go unloved and no part of her can go untouched when you love every inch of her. Cherish her and go to war for her. Know that the enemy lusts after her, but never release what they long for you to let go.

If thy wife is overweight, jealous, insecure, rebellious, loud, arrogant, violent, etc., then one must be patient, pray for wisdom to deal with her issues, and have the faith to know that My Lord can and will change your situation. He knows which circumstances to put in one's life that will change their mind and attitude. My Lord will work all things out for your good. Don't give Him a deadline to resolve your problems, but be patient and persevere through the storm and watch My Lord make it good. Don't murmur, don't complain, be strong and give Him praise. Have faith and put in work. Always nourish and cherish thy woman. Be stronger than her and let your soul love her. If she's acting malicious, render good to all her evil. Bless her if she curses thee. If she behaves or speaks unwisely don't feed into her foolishness. In the process of time the fruit of love that resides in you will increase, and thou shall always have more love to give her.

My Lord manifested that His Church would be cleansed and without flaw. He wants it spotless and a man should feel the same way about his woman. He should want his woman inwardly and outwardly. He should want her without spot or wrinkle, always at her best because she is his Glory. You receive praise when your woman is on point! Foremost, she should be beautiful inwardly and the outward beauty will automatically manifest. Thou must cultivate thy woman, help strengthen her Spirit, and build her mind by giving her understanding and by watering her with the Word of My Lord. The Word will wash her heart and set her apart. Let her soak in the presence of God and watch her be transformed into a melody from Heaven. She will be a stronger woman and a better wife because of her abiding in Christ. She shall bring forth the fruits of life. If she needs to gain or lose weight, then exercise her body. For her body is thy body. Wash, dry, massage, and lubricate her body daily, keep it clean and altogether lovely and walk in the beauty of holiness. Give her what she needs which is the strength of a man. Get stronger and put thy foot down. Be stern with her when need be and smoothly place her in order. If she's a godly woman, she will respect and love to obey thee.

A man must seek out wisdom; for it is by wisdom a house is built. He must be patient, gentle, romantic, very affectionate, decisive, cool, and most of all walk in the fear of My Lord. Pay the price that needs to be paid in order to have a fruitful and lasting relationship with thy spouse. Become a MAN and put foolishness behind you.

For God so loved the world, that he gave his only begotten Son, that whosoever believeth in him should not perish, but have everlasting life.(John 3:16)

Look as the sacrifice God made for us by giving us his Son in spite of our wretchedness. He don't allow the accusation of the devil prevent him from loving us. In spite of our wickedness, He stayed in one mind by not allowing anything to stop him from saving and blessing us. Men we art to be the same with our wives which is immoveable. Nothing or no one should cause you to sway from her or lead thee to disrespect her. Regardless of what's done to entice you to abuse, cheat, and disrespect or dishonor thy woman, don't consent to it. Never do what your enemies desire to have you do. The same way God SO loved the world that He gave His only begotten son, so shall a man SO love his wife. When the enemy persecutes the relationship and throws her past in thy face, reminds you of her mistakes, and falsely accuses her of things, tell them SO. So means despite the rumors, the lies, the gossip, her condition, her past, and who doesn't accept her, you will love her anyway. Family and friends might not like her but SO! A man should SO Love his woman that it doesn't make a difference about her past, who talks about her, who don't like her, how she looks, and/or regardless of the issues in her life, you'll love her anyway and stand with her through the storms.

Understand everything she is, every part of her body, her thoughts, her tears, her history, her possessions, her finances, and her faults belong to thee. The stronger you get, the stronger she becomes because your love strengthens her. Never be ashamed of her; never be afraid to take her places. Those who don't accept her have denied you. Bear your cross with her, forgive her when she makes mistakes and remember not her sins anymore. Sow great measures of love into her, pour thy heart, body, and soul into her, give her quality time and overflow her life with the abundance of joy, peace, and goodness, be merciful to her. A man that profess to love for his woman but he's verbally, mentally, and/or physically abusing her, is far from being a man. His acts of hatred expose the love his mouth professes to have for her to be lies. Men if you're hating on your woman let hate go immediately, meaning cease from doing her any evil. At times when thy woman acts as though she is thy enemy, love her as thine enemy. Love overcomes every obstacle and situation. Love will hold on to her after her family and friends have forsaken her. Love will stand by her while everything else around her hides. Loving her will cause your enemies to hate you more seeing that they can't separate you from her, therefore, increase their hatred and love her all the more. You love her much when you correct her. Therefore, diligently tell her to abase herself every time she exalts herself. Be willing to forgive her seven times seventy. As long as she doesn't cross the line, which is sleeping with another man, don't ever think about putting her away. Always give her good understanding of why you do what you do and why you feel the way you feel. Never despise or offend her, but love her so much that her soul begins to melt each time she enters thy presence. Make it easy for her to open her heart and to share her wants, dreams, and all her secrets with you. She should be willing to give all that is within her possessions to you. Be strong and SO Love Her.

FEED HER SOUL

God has given the man the responsibility of not harming but loving, providing, guiding, nourishing, and teaching the woman. Men, this is why it's important that in all thy getting, get understanding because as a man thou must give thy wife knowledge of the Word of God. Understanding is wisdom, therefore, the more understanding you give her, the wiser she will become. You are the primary tool God is using to mold her into what He has predestined her to be. Therefore, earnestly pray for wisdom because it is the Wisdom of God that will bring her into maturity. For the key to happiness is Wisdom. The wiser you become the happier you'll be. She will be a crown of Glory to thee. A man or woman without understanding is a fool and fools only awaken to shame. Men without understanding do not know how to cultivate a woman. He doesn't nurture her with the wisdom she needs to grow stronger and wiser in Christ. The Greek word for nourish is "ektrepho" which means to rear up to maturity to cherish or train; bring up. Therefore, As Christ nourishes His Church so should a man nourish his wife.

LET THE WOMAN LEARN IN SILENCE WITH ALL SUBJECTION. BUT I SUFFER A WOMAN NOT TO TEACH, NOR TO USURP AUTHORITY OVER A MAN, BUT TO BE IN SILENCE. (1TIMOTHY 2: 11, 12)

A woman must know where she stands and not exalt herself against the knowledge of Jesus Christ. The Word of God instructs her neither to teach nor to be in authority over a man. God has made man stronger than the woman and gave him domination. In First Timothy it is clearly written that a woman should learn in silence from a man with all subjection. Many women have a problem with being in subjection to a man. The word obey is not received at all by them. Many are lifted with pride and feel that a man can't tell them anything, and that they only need a man for sex. Some of them don't need a man for that. That is a dangerous attitude for any of them to have and every woman that thinks that way is in direct rebellion to the Word of God. However, many of them are the first ones to scream how saved, sanctified, and Holy Ghost filled they are.

Many husbands and wives war over what Church to attend. Neither one likes each other's Church. Therefore, many husbands and wives go to Church alone because they refuse to attend one another's Church. First of all, the woman should follow her husband. Though she might not like the Church that her husband attends, be it the people, it's too small, it's too big, or she's not being fed, whatever her reasons are, it's inexcusable. If that's where the Spirit of God is leading him, she must deny herself and bear her cross. First of all, God has called many of us to a higher level and will sometimes send you to a certain place not to be ministered to, but to minister. Secondly, a woman should never have to solely rely on her pastor or bishop to feed or teach her the Word. It's her husband's responsibility to teach her the Word of God, and any Christian woman that is considering getting married to a man that has no knowledge of God and can't cultivate her according to the Word of God, is making a BIG mistake. However, if she's married to man of God and if she values her pastor or church more than her marriage and the word of God, she's out of order and needs to repent.

A man who prays and obeys My Lord will always have more to teach his wife because God will constantly increase his knowledge and understanding. As he waters his wife, the Lord will water him. The heart is the storage place for the Word, so if the Word dwell in you richly, it shall flow out of you naturally. Some may think you talk too much, but as long as you are speaking life and not talking about yourself, gossiping, or vain talking, then your lips are supposed to feed many. If you don't have sound doctrine to feed your wife then you're not doing something right because

My Lord gives wisdom, knowledge, understanding, and joy to a man that is good in His sight. Therefore, a good man will always have something to impart to his woman because he is in contact with God, having ears to hear what thus saith the Lord and

A MAN THAT HEARETH SPEAKETH CONSTANTLY (PROVERBS 21:28)

A man needs his woman to be quiet while he's nourishing her with the Word of God. He needs her undivided attention as he reads the Word to her. Her silence is a show of respect. Respect is an issue in many marriages. When a woman doesn't respect her husband she won't receive the Word from him. She'll take his understanding of it for granted and will be quick to think or say that he doesn't know anything he is talking about. Until respect is established, then will the Word be honored out of his mouth and He can begin to feed her soul. Before a man begins to feed her soul, he needs to first ensure that he has her undivided attention. He should eliminate all distractions. The T.V., radio, computer, and telephones should be turned off. She should sit silently because attempting to teach her while she's talking, moving, or rambling around is not having her under subjection. She shouldn't do anything unless permitted. For example, many women in the process of their man trying to show them something, will be rambling around and saying something like "continue talking baby" while looking for her keys, or while dialing a number on the phone she's says, "go ahead" claiming she can hear everything he is saying. Whether she is quiet or not, isn't the only problem, for she might be quiet, however, she's roaming and doing whatever she wants to, and in that case, she is out of control. Her moving around is not only a distraction but it's disrespectful. Her husband will often have to repeat himself. She's not honoring her man and there is no glory in that.

Many women behave unwisely and will not submit to the truth. The Gospel teaches that a woman should not usurp authority over a man. Therefore, every woman who is calling the shots in the house is out of order. It is a sin for a woman to dress like a man; therefore, every woman (figuratively speaking) that is "wearing the pants" in the house, is in sin. Every woman in My Lord, who will not submit to her husband in everything, and has an independent attitude, or perhaps feels because she makes more money or has more degrees than her husband, that she is the head of the house, is out of order. Any woman who has been in the Church longer than their husband and feels because of that he can't show or teach her anything in the Word of God is out of order. My Lord can always give a man quick understanding and will give a man who humbles himself quick understanding of His Word so that he may teach his wife. By wisdom is a house built; not by education or money. A man who's submitted to the Word of God is lead by the wisdom of God and shall by faith and patience establish his house. Women, respect thy husband! He should have a good time loving you. Why make it hard for him to teach and lead you? Thou have nothing to gain by acting unruly. Don't behave as though you're in competition with him. A man should engage in spiritual warfare for his wife and not on her.

OBEY THEM THAT HAVE THE RULE OVER YOU, AND SUBMIT YOURSELVES: FOR THEY WATCH FOR YOUR SOULS, AS THEY MAY DO IT WITH JOY, AND NOT WITH GRIEF: FOR THAT IS UNPROFITABLE FOR YOU. (HEBREWS 13: 17)

SHE ME

HE THAT LOVETH HIS WIFE LOVETH HIMSELF. (EPHESIANS 5:28)

In the beginning Adam and Eve's relationship was altogether lovely, they lived joyfully as one in the presence of My Lord. They were naked and not ashamed, and their fruits of righteousness would have never withered away because sin wasn't in the world. However, it would have multiplied throughout time. As they grew older their love would have grown stronger. Their peace would have become greater; their joy would've become fuller, etc. They would have never grown weary of loving one another. For My Lord made them two tight when he made them one, now how tighter can two become? He didn't put them near each other, he joined them together, for they were never considered to be two, but were made one flesh.

When Adam saw Eve, he said "WO" for he had seen a modified reflection of himself and called her Woman. For she was not only part of him, she was the feminine expression of him. She was beautiful in his eyes. She was the first one of God's creation that he could identify and communicate with. He had finally seen someone of his nature that he could share his most intimate thoughts with. She was bone of his bone, and flesh of his flesh. **She-Me** was his attitude. They were made in the image and likeness of God; therefore, they were like each other in nature.

All those who are seeking their soul mate should pray to My Lord to bring them that one that they can identify with, the one he or she is compatible with. When any man finds a woman to become one with, **She Me,** should become his concept because the moment My Lord put them together, they have become One. Neither of them can live as though they are single entities or think independently of the other. They must think as one, together forever. They shouldn't be able to imagine themselves without each other. When you see a man without his wife or vice versa, you are only seeing half the picture. Any godly man who is considering getting married, but can't say **She-Me** about her, should reconsider.

When a man loves his woman he's blessing his own soul. Everything he does for her, he's doing for himself. Therefore, if he wants the best for himself, he'll only want the best for his woman, understanding that everything about her reflects on him. For **She-Me** should sound from his lips every time he looks and speaks of her. If anyone disrespects her, they are disrespecting him **(ME)**. Every one that lust for her is lusting for **Me**. **She** is the part of **Me** no man better ever lay his hands on and **She** is the part of **Me** every man should long to have but can't touch. **She** is **Me** from the top of her head to the bottom of her feet. Everything inside and outside of her is adored by **ME**. When the enemy persecutes and afflicts her, lies on her and to her, he is not only doing it to **Me,** but he is tempting **Me** to war in the flesh.

For those who don't want her around, don't want **Me** around. Places where neither **She** nor **Me** are welcome, we don't enter. Family, friends, or whoever don't accept her, don't accept **Me**. Those who are jealous of her are jealous of **Me**, those who despise her are despising **Me**, and those who bless her are blessing **Me**. **She** is never separated or apart from **Me**. When **She's** not with **Me** in body, **She's** with **Me** in heart. Therefore, we are constantly together. Her heart, her mind, her body, her soul is deeply loved by **Me**. Her tears, her fears, her emotions, her mistakes are medicated by **Me**. For every step **She** takes is with **Me,** and we can't do anything without Christ. For in all of our ways we acknowledge him and he directs our path. For our life is Christ. We love JESUS, for he is our Lord.

My wife is my first ministry. For **She** saith her days are incomplete if she hasn't made love to **Me** morning, noon, and night. Her lips love to caress every inch of **Me**. **She** only desires **Me** mentally, physically, and spiritually. For **She** wants **Me** only and **She** loves making **Me** happy. **She** doesn't give ear to fools who speak badly of **Me**. **She** is so hot for **Me**; it torments the mind of my enemies. For **She** gives no space to them. They hate that **She's** with **Me** because **She** is a crown of Glory to **Me**. For **She** feeds **Me** strength making **Me** ten times stronger. My enemies wish **She** would turn from **Me** but her love falls deep in **Me**. **She** will never do my enemies will. **She** will never leave nor forsake **Me**. For **She** can always rely on **Me** and **She** does trust **Me**. **She** loves **Me** like no one has ever loved **Me** before. **She** doesn't remind **Me** of my mistakes, and **She** treats **Me** like a King. **She** is there for **Me** and **She** helps **Me**. How **She** feels means so much to **Me**. When **She** cries her tears water **Me**. When things get too heavy for her, **She** tosses the excess weight on **Me**. **She** leans on **Me**. For **She** has learned and knows everything about **Me**. **She's** revealed all her secrets to **Me**, and refuses to ever keep anything from **Me**. **She's** never afraid to tell **Me** anything and **She** never disrespects **Me**. **She** calls **Me** her best friend.

For we are One in Christ, and that's how My Lord blessed us to be. Daily **She** prays for **Me**. **She** will go all out for **Me** and **She** shall never hurt **Me**. **She** shall do **Me** good and not evil all the days her of life. **She** is a virtuous woman. **She** is a joy to **Me**. **She** wakes **Me** early with tender kisses. My Lord has blessed the fruits of her body, and **She** has **Me** to taste of her sweetness all the day. **She** feeds **Me** dessert. **She** is a healthy choice. **She** is the depth of **Me**. To touch her is to touch the deepest and most intimate part of **Me**. Thou can't know her unless thou first come to know **Me**. For it is impossible to know her apart from **Me** because we are so tight in Christ, My Lord. **She** only hopes the best for **Me**. **She** wants **Me** strong and my strength is firm. She likes **Me** to be stern with her. **She** likes for **Me** to put my foot down when need be. **She** loves for **Me** to be in control. **She** is everything a man hopes for in a woman. **She** can't get enough of **Me**, and daily **She** expresses how **She** yearns for more of **Me.** For her desires for **Me** continuously increases. **She** is addicted to **Me.** Her body fiends for **Me,** and her mind can't stay off **Me.**

    She loves **Me** without hypocrisy. **She** spoils **Me** and **She** wants **Me** tight at all times. For the way **She** cares for **Me** blows every one's mind and the depths of her love for **Me** is unspeakable. There is never too much time, money, or love **She** can give **Me. She** loves to listen to **Me. She** loves for **Me** to speak knowledge, wisdom, and understanding into her soul. For **She** loves to learn from **Me. She** gives **Me** an obedient ear, **She** learns in silence. **She** is the one handcrafted by God to handle all of **Me.** For **She** is no joke and **She** tells people that see **Me** that "**He** is **Me**" **She** is not to be tampered with. A woman was made for a man to love, and when he cherishes her, he is doing good to his own soul. If **"She-Me"** is not being echoed in his heart then one might question his love. If he loves himself and keeps himself together, then he should only want the same for his woman. However, if he hates himself, it shall manifest in how he treats his woman, he must repent and let hate go. Same goes for a woman. She should love her man in pureness of heart. Her love should be unquestionable. A wise woman, who experiences the depth of her man's love, will want to love him more. She should be willing to obey her man in everything, and trusting that the Spirit of God is leading him. When the man obeys God the woman better obey him. If the woman doesn't obey him, he must not trip off time, and be patient as My Lord puts his house in line with **She-Me** as his philosophy despite the struggles he and his woman might face. Everything about her he should love and those things that are not of God that he doesn't like, he should pray and wait on My Lord to change, but **She-Me** should be his philosophy from beginning till the end.

PROVIDE FOR HER

But if any provide not for his own, and especially for those of his own house, he hath denied the faith, and is WORSE than an infidel. (1 Timothy 5:8)

Husbands you are the providers for the house. Your wife should never have to argue with you over you not working because if you are a man that believes in God, surely you know if you have a wife and/or kids you need a JOB. Your first priority is to provide for your family, so a man works as much as necessary in order to supply the things that his family needs. This by no means is suggesting that a woman shouldn't work a secular job because if a man needs assistance financially, that's what she is there for, to be his HELP MEET. Also, a man can lose his job at anytime and/or go thru a storm and he may need his woman to pull some extra weight, as he diligently tries to get back on his feet, but a woman should never have to baby sit a man. Any man that watches his wife put in all the work while he sits back and does nothing is far from being a man; therefore, husbands make sure you're not taking advantage of your wives. She is there to help you, not do the task for you, so don't be the type of lazy no good man who only sits back and enjoy the fruits of all her labor. Your her husband not her Pimp. If you don't want to work, not only do you not deserve a wife you don't deserve a meal.

For even when we were with you, this we commanded you, that if any would not work, neither should he eat.(2 Thessalonians 3:10)

Some men use the excuse that their not working a secular job, so that they can dedicate all their time working on their dreams of being a comedian, writer, singer, rapper, actor, etc. Men it's good that you have a vision and always work towards that vision. If your wife can hold things down financially while you WORK on accomplishing your dreams, by all means chase your dream. However, if she can't bear the financial burden alone then don't be dead weight to her, but do what's required of you and help bear the burdens.

As a man you must not only tend to the natural things your family need, but most importantly the spiritual things your household need. Shelter, food, clothes, water are some of the natural needs you must provide. Love, wisdom, knowledge, understanding, faith, patience, etc are the Spiritual elements you must provide. If a man provide the spiritual elements needed, he'll never lack anything in the natural.

DON'T BE GREEDY

Money problems in marriage often stem from greed. It is one the major reasons many are in debt today. It has been one of the primary causes of many divorces. Many husbands and wives have walked away from another, betrayed each other and killed. Greed causes one's eyes to be bigger than their budget, thus, lead them to buy things they cannot afford. Many charge up credit cards, take out personal loans, write bad checks, pond their car title, etc. so that they may buy things they want. They pay high interest rates on these things; therefore, they're actually paying a lot more than what the item is worth. Yet, the very things they're going broke for in hopes of improving their life, ends up being a headache because they spend the rest of their life struggling to dig themselves out of the pits of debt.

He that is greedy of gain troubleth his own house; but he that hateh gifts shall live (Pro. 15:27)

Example, a woman once wanted a new cell-phone because her screen on her phone had a few cracks. Instead of purchasing a cell phone she could afford, she wanted the top notch cell phone that cost $499. She could have easily bought a much less expensive cell phone until she was able to buy the one she wanted, but "in her mind" she thought why not just get the phone her eyes desired. Unknown to her husband, she decided to pond the car title of the only car in the household because the New Year was approaching and she figured she would repay the loan immediately with her income tax check. Title Pawn gave her $900 for her car title and required her to repay 1050 back; therefore, in essence it was $150 more she had to pay for the phone making the total amount $650 plus taxes. She got the phone she wanted, but when it came time to pay off her debt IRS did an audit on her. They discovered she had been lying on her taxes and withheld her check from her, so she could not pay back the title loan. The day Title Pawn came and redeemed the car, is the day it is revealed to her Husband all that she had done. His temperature begins to boil because they have a 2yr old child and he is the only one currently working in the household. They both are in school and now their only means of transportation has been taken from them. He stop speaking peaceably to her for days. Frustrations and stress floods there household because now they must not rely on public transportation, but they only have two weeks to come up with $1500 to redeem their car or they will lose it. They borrowed the money from family and friends and got their car back. In conclusion, a cell phone cost her $1100, unnecessary stress and almost the lost of her family. Her first mistake was that she didn't discuss anything with her husband. Secondly, she didn't need a new phone because the one she had still worked, but Her greed troubled her house.

One way to help resolve some of the many money problems in your marriage is to stop being greedy. Tear up all credit cards and/or keep one for emergency purposes only because if it's not an emergency don't borrow money for something you don't NEED. Don't gamble or risk losing what you NEED for something you don't NEED. Be content with the things you have and patiently wait until you can afford to purchase the things you want. If you can't buy it cash don't buy it. Don't allow the enemy to deceive you with the credit trap because good credit bad credit are just spruced up terms he uses in lieu of good servant/ bad servant and rather good are bad the bottom line you're a servant.

The rich ruleth over the poor, and the borrower is the servant to the lender. (proverbs 22:7)

God promised us if we obey him that we shall lend and not borrow. So husbands and wives if you want to be the head and not the tail regardless of how great your credit is don't borrow money. Be content with the things you have and wait until you can afford to buy whatever you want without financing it though others. Example, if you have a reliable vehicle that's paid for, it would be unwise of you to trade that vehicle in and finance a brand new luxury car. Why put yourself back into debt? What if you lose your job? The peace of having something paid for is far greater than having something unpaid for because if you ever lose your job or decrease in income, you don't deal with the stress of trying to make those payments. For this very reason many are without a car because they minded high things. The benefits of making wise choices are priceless compared to the grief greed can cause you. Control your appetite because in this life there will always be things that you want to buy and those that have no control over their lust runs up mountains of debt. They will rob peter to pay Paul. They get behind on their mortgage, car notes, utility bills, medical bills, etc They'll skip paying those things in order to buy things they want and the end result is more debt, therefore, it is vital for husbands and wives to bring their appetite under subjection

Be of the same mind one toward another. Mind not high things, but condescend to men of low estate. Be not wise in your own conceits. (Romans 12:16)

The way to control your appetite is to change your way of thinking. Stop believing that happiness, peace, self-worth etc. can only be found when you're standing on top of the World because what does it profit a man who gains the whole world, but lose his own soul? People who calculate their worth by the things they possess, spend their life chasing money by any means necessary. If it doesn't make dollars, it doesn't make sense to them. The things some of them do for money are the reasons why they don't have joy, peace, etc. Understand, High priced things don't give you a better life or marriage. Only the things you SOW into your marriage can improve your marriage. There are billions of people in poverty, yet many of them are happy because many of them have learned to be thankful to God just for being ALIVE. They are thankful for peace of mind. They are happy for good health and/or grateful for food and clothing. Men of low estate don't care about owning a big house, they are thankful just to have shelter. If husbands and wives were to condescend to men of low estate the things that they don't have will never come in between them because they'll be too grateful and too busy celebrating over the things they do have. When you mind high things you will complain if you not have what others have, but when you condescend to men of low estate you'll recognize that their many that don't have near as much as you have and you'll be very thankful for what you do have. People's financial situation always changes, money comes and money goes, so don't set your heart on riches. Someone whose broke today can be rich tomorrow, someone whose rich today can be broke tomorrow, so however your financial situation shifts, let your heart be fixed trusting in the Lord.

Labour not to be rich: cease from thine own wisdom. Wilt thou set thine eyes upon that which is not? For riches certainly make themselves wings; they will fly away as an eagle toward heaven (Proverbs 23:4)

Wives, don't act as if your husband can't PAY FOR EVERYTHING, that he's not fulfilling his responsibility as a man. You were created to help him in every area of his life, so assist him financially when need be. Don't attempt to make him feel small, cheap, or not man enough for you when he can't afford to finance the things that you desire for him to because it exposes you to be the type of foolish woman that is bought with a price. His love is for you not measured by the amount of money he spends on you. No man can feel secure with a woman who he knows he's buying her love because he understands that Money can't purchase loyalty.

Women with a gold-digger mentality makes men that can't afford to purchase their love, feel less than a man. This is the main reason why simple minded men resort to making dishonest gains in order to keep from being rejected and despised in the eyes of these gold digging whores. This should not be the case. Men, The Lord wants you to make an honest living, so in spite of that woman's attitude, complaints, criticism, etc don't do anything illegal or anything that endangers neither you nor your family in efforts to provide for your family. Why put yourself in that position that can cause you to be taken away from them or them from you? Too many men do things such as sell drugs, steal, commit armed robbery, check fraud, prostitute themselves, their wife and/or kids etc. as a means of provision and such forms of dishonest living is the cause many are incarcerated and/or dead today. It's depressing for a man to sit inside of a jail cell with another man for years or for life, knowing that his wife and/or kids or either been taken care of by another Man or left alone to live without him. Refrain from all forms of dishonest living.

Recompense to no man evil for evil. Provide things—honest in the sight of all men.—(Romans 12:17)

THE LOVE OF MONEY

For the love of money is the root of all evil: which while some coveted after, they have erred from the faith, and pierced themselves through with many sorrows. (1 Timothy 6:10)

Money is not the problem it's the LOVE for money that causes people problems. Lies, betrayal, murder, back stabbings, infidelity and many more evils that husband and wives has committed against each other all for the Love of Money. Many relationships have come to a bitter end because money was coveted after or they allowed financial distresses to come in-between them. Both men and women have walked away from their spouses not because their spouses didn't treat them right, but because in their eyes their mate wasn't bringing enough bread(money) to the table. Their heart lusted for more and in wanting instant gratification they fell into the net of the enemy who used the deceitfulness of riches to seduce them into violating their marital vows they made to God. They were tested to reveal what was in their heart and in failing that test, it exposed they valued money over the commandments of God. Thus, showing them that they honored God with their mouths, but their heart was far from him. Had they served the Lord knowing that He supplies their needs, they would have not allowed money to divide them. They would have exercised godliness with contentment while patiently waiting on God to bless them, however, they didn't do the will of God, instead they obeyed the will of dirty money. The deceitfulness of riches caused them to believe that they would enjoy & be better off with the luxuries that money would bring them, ABOVE the peace and blessings that obedience to the WORD would bring them. Therefore, they brought sorrows and troubles upon their own soul.

No man can serve two masters: for either he will hate the one, and love the other; or else he will hold to the one, and despise the other. Ye cannot serve God and mammon. (Matthew 6:24)

God is your provider so some-ones income should never be an excuse to marry or divorce them. If you married him or her and they weren't making much at the time you said, "I DO" to love them, till death do you part, you surely can't turn around and use

171

the excuse of them having insufficient funds to divorce them. Their low income didn't stop you from marrying them, so why would it cause you to divorce them. If a man or woman can't afford to buy you certain things that doesn't mean he or she doesn't love you because the quality nor the measure of love isn't determined by how much someone makes or spends on you. Contrary to the way many think, it doesn't take money to love someone. However, a person that doesn't know what love is won't know how to love regardless of how much their net worth is. If the quality of love was equivalent to the amount money a person makes then why are so many rich people unhappily married or divorced? Understand, that it's Love and not money that worketh no ills; therefore, just because a person has money, their money won't prevent them from doing things that could deeply hurt you. Only love can prevent them from doing things that would hurt you. If love isn't in their heart, he or she may buy you a car, house, diamond ring and everything, but that doesn't mean that they won't lie, cheat, betray, or abuse you, etc. because they will.

A woman that lacks understanding would walk away from A poor man that walks in love or make her husband feel inferior to other men that are currently make more money than he is. However, more money doesn't mean better or more love. Money can give you material luxury, but money can't give you the luxury that love gives to your soul. Meaning money can give you the big house, nice car, expensive clothes, and worldwide tours, but money can't give you the guidance, security, companionship, peace, joy, goodness, gentleness, etc., that love provides to your soul. A person may be able to buy you the world, but if their spirit is not of love, you will not be able to enjoy the world as long as he or she is in it. Understand, that the spirit of the giver is very important and God loves a cheerful giver. A person that loves you will find pleasure in giving to you freely. However, many people give reluctantly or with the wrong intent. You can give all your possessions to feed the poor, but if you have not love, you profit nothing from it. Many will give you things with the expectation of receiving from you in return. When a person gives in the attitude that you owe them something in return, it was not given freely. They used their money to purchase your time, sex, money, favors, in other-words they're trying to barter with you. They're not taking you out, or helping you out financially without getting anything in return because in their eyes you would be a bad investment. They have a "cash for azz" mentality. If you're not giving up some form of sex then they're not spending any money on you.

You should always appreciate what a person gives you and never take it for granted. Whether a person gives little or much, if they did it from the pureness of heart, you should be grateful and respect it. Husband and wives should give freely to one another with the understanding that the material things they give to one another, isn't more valuable than the love they should have for each other.

What is your spouse presence in your life worth to you? Hopefully you married your spouse because you found love in them and if you've found "love" in them, what would you risk losing it for? Would you jeopardize losing it for a certain dollar amount, material things, a cheap thrill, a drug, etc.? Many have betrayed the love of their spouse for one of those things and now regret it because they realized they lost everything. Love is the greatest of all things, so if you've found love in them only a fool that doesn't know the value of love would walk away from them. All of the money in the world can't give you what love can give you. The security and peace that it provides cannot be provided by anything money can buy; therefore, before you allow someone to use their money, beauty, material things, etc to seduce you to walk away from love, calculate how much you will be losing and ask yourself is it worth it? For when love joins two people together hell and high waters can't break them apart.

MANY WATERS CANNOT QUENCH LOVE, NEITHER CAN THE FLOODS DROWN IT, IF A MAN WOULD GIVE ALL THE SUBSTANCE HOUSE FOR LOVE, IT WOULD UTTERLY BE CONTEMNED (Solomon 8:7)

If you love one another, money cannot divide you because your love for one another will cause you to tackle all your money problems together. Trust God as your provider and know that it doesn't matter if you lose your job, nor does it matter how much money you make on paper because hr shall supply all of your needs. Wives when your husband can't afford to pay all the bills, escort you to expensive restaurants, take you on vacation, or buy you all the things your eyes lust for, don't attempt to lower his self esteem by saying demeaning things. He may not have the money to do the things you would like for him to do, but if that same man is honest and longsuffering with you, if he is good to you and does things you ask of him to do in good spirits, if he gives you the attention, support and encouragement you need, if he prays for you and with you, if he feeds you wisdom and truth, if he secures your heart by walking trustworthy. If he is faithful, and hasn't made you feel intimidated or threatened by anything or anyone. If he is gentle with you, respect and honors you, if he give you companionship and is compassionate towards you when you're ill, if he helps you carry your burdens and has been nothing but a blessing to you, if he protects you and laid down his life for you, you would be a foolish woman to walk away from Him. Likewise men, if your wife doesn't work a secular job that doesn't mean she's eating the bread of idleness. If she is good home-keeper, if she arises early and makes you breakfast, prepares your lunch, have your dinner ready, wash and iron your clothes, submissive to your will, runs errands for you, nourishing the kids naturally and spiritually, if she's adorned with a meek and quiet spirit, non-resistant to your love and affection, etc. it would be very unwise of you to betray her love for another woman just become that other women could be more beneficial to you financially.

Men and women if your spouse betrayed your love for a fool who seduced them with money, pray for their soul and WATCH! Anytime someone chooses money over the will of God, they've made a grave mistake. Those who have betrayed their spouse for money pierced themselves through with many sorrows. The grass may have appeared greener on the other side, but once they stepped on Satan's lawn they walked on to a field loaded with landmines. Understand whosoever seduces a married man or woman regardless of how rich or poor they are, has no fear of God because the commandment of God is not to covet thy neighbor's wife. Any who doesn't fear God hasn't begun to be wise. The Enemy always has his way of making it appear as though he is a better choice through the art of seduction, that's why it's important to walk by faith and not by sight because in the end the truth will always prevail. Don't let the deceitfulness of riches deceive and blind you. Keep this in mind...

BETTER IS A DINNER OF HERBS WHERE LOVE IS, THAN A STALLED OX AND HATRED THEREWITH. (PROVERBS 15:17)

In other words, it's much better to abide in the presence of loving man eating ramen noodles, than to be with a hateful man eating T-bone steaks. Don't give more respect to a person solely because he has more money or because he can buy you things and take you places that your spouse who truly love you can't afford to do at that time. The Devil maybe offering you a more expensive plate, but it doesn't mean it's a healthier choice. The issues you would have to deal with, when you involve yourself with anyone that doesn't have love inside of them, is far greater than anything you'll experience with someone walking in love. Examine your heart because if your heart is pure you should desire to be where ever love reside. There is nothing anyone should be able to offer you or buy you that should cause you to depart from love because the peace and joy that loves gives you is priceless. Also, understand that the person who gives you five dollars can be giving you more than the one who is giving you five thousand. Jesus taught a parable that the woman who gave him two pennies gave him more than those who gave from the abundance of their treasures because she gave out of debt. Though the dollar amount was smaller, her sacrifice was bigger because she gave him all she had, so just because a person has spent more doesn't mean he or she gave you more than the one who spent less. It's not about the value of the gift but about the heart of the giver. Love is much more valuable than money; love gives you profitable things that money can never supply. A man with no fear of God may purchase you a $5,000 dollar bed, but he'll make you feel like a $5 dollar whore. Yet, a man that fears God, may only be able to afford to purchase you a $5 pillow, but he'll make you feel like your priceless.

BETTER IS LITTLE WITH <u>THE FEAR OF THE LORD</u> THAN GREAT TREASURE AND TROUBLE THEREWITH. (PROVERBS 15:16)

Too many relationships are destroyed because of money problems. Insufficient funds in your bank account shouldn't cause a deficit in your love for one another, but many couples are practically slashing each other's throat over their financial situation. Complaining and fighting each other over money won't solve your money issues, so don't let where you at financially cause confusion and strife between you two. Be content, make a plan, work diligently together towards it and wait on God to bless the work of your hands. The race isn't given to the swift, so don't envy others who appear to have more than you because regardless of how much people possess, the abundance of life isn't determined by the abundance of things. Many that are rich have poor marriages and many that are poor have rich marriages. The difference is the rich trust in their money, so they are very poor in faith, but the poor trust in God being rich in faith. Although the rich have riches since their without faith it's impossible for them to please God. They have money but they have no peace. Understand, it's important for you to seek God first because as long as you have faith and fear God, you are a lot better off than those who have more things but don't have him. It's far better to live in a small apartment with peace and love than to have a big mansion with no peace in it. Big Timers may brag on their big money, big car, big house, and how their doing big things, but they won't tell you about their big problems that comes with their big money. Please understand as long as you have God you got all you need to be happy with. If you have little money, little place, little car, etc. know that if you are faithful in little, God shall bless thee with much more in due time. And you'll know it's coming from God because whatever God bless you with, the blessing that he gives you will make you rich. It will make you rich in mind, body, soul, and spirit. You will be rich in his Word, rich in his goodness and mercy because you're rich in Faith!

THE BLESSING OF THE LORD, IT MAKETH RICH, AND HE ADDETH NO SORROW TO IT (Proverbs 10:22)

A marriage is rich when two people are truly happy together, their joy is not contingent upon where they live, where they go, who they are around, nor how much money they have, because in spite of people, places and things, they are happy just being together and will make the best out of everything. The time they spend together is more important than anything because they experience love, joy, and peace just being in each other's presence. They don't have to leave the house in order to have a good time because they have good times in the house. They understand it's not about the size of their house or car, but the size of their heart. Couples that don't understand this don't enjoy one another; most of them don't even like their spouse. They're only married on paper. When they try to do things to spice up their relationship it won't work because when you don't like one another, you may go to a fun places together, but you won't have fun being there together because you're there with someone you don't like.

Couples should be in one mind, one Spirit, serving one Lord, and abiding in the presence of God, forbearing, and loving one another with the love of Christ. Regardless of their conditions, finances, and health, if their love is real, it can endure, bear, and believe all things are possible through Christ who is able to deliver, strengthen, and make whole. Love is the greatest of all; therefore, Love is the only thing husbands and wives should give to each other. Trials may be lengthy but love endures it. Trials may get heavy but love can bear it. Trials can raise doubts and stir worries; however, love believeth that the peace of God that passes all understanding shall rule thy hearts and minds. In spite of how long or hard the trial is, love hangs on. Therefore, love one another, stick closely together, and forsake each other not. If you both Love God with all thine heart, soul, mind, and strength, God promises you that regardless of how bad things seems to get, that he will bring something wonderful out of it. So, hold on knowing all things work together for the good for them that love God. For one can chase a thousand, but two can put ten thousand to flight in Christ. Thankfully, a man and his wife are ten times stronger when they're together. Your enemies will flee in seven different ways when you stand as one. Deliverance, healings, and miracles come quicker when couples worship and pray fervently together, so hold on to one another and do not let each other go. With God on your side the enemy isn't capable of cutting you two asunder. You should cry together, laugh together, sleep together, worship God together, inherit the grace of life together, and let nothing or no-one separate what God has joined together.

SOUL OF MAN

AND THE LORD GOD FORMED MAN FROM THE DUST OF THE GROUND AND BREATHED INTO HIS NOSTRILS THE BREATH OF LIFE, AND MAN BECAME A LIVING SOUL. (GENESIS 2:7)

In the beginning when God created Adam he made him from mud and until the breath of God entered into him, he had no life in him. At this stage of development man was irresponsive, unconscious, mute, cold, in other words he was dead. Many women made the mistake of marrying a man in this premature stage. They were deceived because he was a fully developed male. Their fascination over the hunk of a man that God had sculptured him into, sparked strong physical desires for him even to the point of what some call "love at first sight". The moment they laid eyes on him, without even knowing his name they knew he was the ONE. They gave no attention to that fact that he was absent of the breath of life, but being head over hills with his masculinity they rushed into a marriage with a lifeless man and found themselves involved with a man who was irresponsive to their needs. They were completely unaware of the foolish things he was doing. He was a man that showed no real love or desires for them. He is unreasonable and unable to communicate life to them because he had no life in him, thus, they fell in love with a mound of mud.

Wives (husbands) if you're husbands (wives) seems to be comatose, pray and ask God to breathe life into him. Understand it wasn't until after God blew into man's nostrils that man became alive. It wasn't until his Spirit entered man that Man Opened His Eyes to behold the Glory of a woman. This is to say that flesh alone can't love you. It was the soul of Adam and Eve that loved one another and in the beginning sin had no part in them. Adam was made in the image and likeness of God meaning he was a righteousness man. He automatically knew how to love his woman in deed and in truth because by nature he was incapable of thinking evil. He could only do right because his heart was initially made pure.

MY LITTLE CHILDREN, LET US LOVE NOT IN WORD, NIETHER IN TONGUE; BUT IN DEED AND IN TRUTH. (1JOHN 3:18)

You can always tell if a person is real by observing the things they do. Example when Christ manifested in the flesh, He knew many wouldn't believe He was the Son of God. However, He done so many wonderful and powerful works, that he told them if they didn't believe His words to look at his works because those things that he did gave proof that he had to be the Son of God. No man could do what He did unless they came from the Heavenly Father. Likewise, in marriage, when you have doubts about the love your spouse confesses to have for you, just look at their actions because even if they never audibly told you that they loved you, can you clearly see their love? Even when their silent is their love for you obvious? Are the things they do a testimony of their love for you? Ask yourself, are their deed evidence of the love that their mouth confesses it has for you? Do they put in works of love or hate? We are commanded to love neither in word nor in tongue, but to let your works speak for you as Christ did with us. Many couples love one another in words but love is verb(action word). If the love their professing to have for one another isn't visible, then those words of love proceeding out of their mouths although they are smooth as butter they are vain because they are deceitful sweet lies. If you love one another don't love with your mouth but by your deeds. Love requires you to DO something good for them.

Men examine yourself and see exactly what your actions are telling her. If a woman can't tell people about the wonderful things her man has done for her, the sacrifices he's made for her, the wisdom he's imparted into her, the security he's given her, the kindness he's shown her, the patience he's had with her , etc. then it's understandable why people may tell her that she deserves better.

When a man loves his wife he shouldn't ever have to convince her of his love with words because his actions will undeniably reveal his love for her. It will be evident to all that He cherishes her because he'll be nothing but good to her and completely honest with her. Whenever he says to her. "I Love You" his words will only confirm to her what he's already proven to her in his actions. His words will be like sweet melodies in her heart because she knows beyond a shadow of doubt that her man is speaking the truth. Unlike other men, his love isn't in question because he does nothing to make her feel insecure. The way he loves her makes her want to yield every part of herself to him. The warmth of his kiss, the strength in his embrace, the passion of his touch will send chills up and down her spine causing her body to surrender to his will as her lips melt into his. He keeps her in the strength of his right hand. He explores her mind, gets deeply involved in her business, and shows her that he cares about every issue surrounding her. When the soul of man loves his woman the right way, she'll praise God for him because the love she experiences from him will be invigorating to her mind, body and soul. Those who envy her hate hearing about how good her man is to her, but those who are of God are happy she's with a man that has her soul praising God. His love stems from a pure heart; therefore, his love is without abuse, without offense, without malice because his love is harmless. His love is so intense that she feels the thickness of it every time she enters his presence. He prays for her, speak the word to her, and guide her through the journey of life hand joined in hand as Christ guides him. Any thought of hurting her that enters his mind he immediately cast it down because in order to entertain that thought he would have to betray his heart and to betray his own heart is like committing suicide and he loves himself too much to kill himself. His fruits are sweet to her taste and his love only get better to her. His love brightens her countenance and has her giving much thanks to the Most High God for blessing her life with wonderful days and beautiful nights with the soul of a man that she can rest in.

MY SOUL SHALL MAKE HER BOAST IN THE LORD THE HUMBLE SHALL HEAR AND BE GLAD THEREOF. (PSALM 34:2)

King David knew that his soul made his woman scream higher praises to the name of **Jesus!** How he loved her, how he touched her, how he spoke to her, and how he fed her fruits, he was a banner of love over her. He made her feel **GOOD**. His passion and fear of God sanctified him in her eyes. They went to the house of My Lord faithfully and exalted His holy name together. The ways that his soul magnified My Lord through psalm, through harp, through dance, and through his life strengthened his woman to boast in Jesus. His love and fear of God was so strong and clearly seen, that the humble rejoiced when they heard how happy he made her. He praised God from the depths of his soul. Unlike many men King David wasn't afraid to worship God uninhibitedly despite of who was offended by it. Likewise women, a man should be able to testify about your love. If he can't brag on how good you are too him, the sacrifices you made for him, the respect you give him, the patience you've had with him, the way you've held things down for him, the loyalty you've given him, how you're love is like water to a thirsty soul that he can never have enough of, then it's understandable why his associates are telling him that he can find better.

The love you give to another should be pure, so make sure your love for one another is according to truth and sincerity because many couples love for one another is polluted with hypocrisy. They do nice things for each other and speak kindly to one another, but it's the things they do and speak behind each other's back that makes their love hypocritical. For example, a woman may be the bread winner of the house and be a help to

181

her man financially, but if she's complaining the whole the time too others how broke, busted, and weak he is, she's being a hypocrite. Likewise, a man may do nice things and speak sweetly to his woman calling her his "baby cakes" but if he gets around his friends and refers to his wife as his "female dog" and tell them she isn't anything but a headache to him, he's being a hypocrite. Marriage is an exclusive relationship, so regardless of how wonderful you are to one another on the surface, if you're indulging in secret love affairs you're not loving one another according to the truth. Love won't backstab you but a hypocrite will, so let not your love be with hypocrisy but love in deed and in truth. If your mouth is confessing love to them, but your actions are hateful toward them, "in-deed" you have lied to them. Every couple needs to think of their deeds towards each other daily. Do you really love your spouse? Have you shown them your love in deeds and in truth, or just in words? Does the record speak for itself?

FOR A LYING TONGUE HATETH THOSE THAT ARE AFFLICTED BY IT. (PROVERBS 26:28)

There is a right and many wrong ways to love someone and The Lord wants you to love in truth not in lies. To love your spouse in truth is to love your spouse not in your way, but in the way the Word instructs you to and He commands a man to love his wife the way Christ so love the Church and for a wife to obey her husband in everything, in doing so you abide in the truth. If a man dwell with his woman according to knowledge, give her honor, nourish and cherish her soul, making sacrifices for her, letting her breast satisfy him at all times, being ravished with her love always, and living joyfully with her, he is loving her in truth. If a woman adorns herself with a meek and quiet spirit, look well to the ways of her household; be in subjection to her own husband in everything, only good to him and not evil, secure his heart, etc. she is loving her man in truth. If you can justify your actions in the

Word of God then your actions are done according to truth. For the Word of God counsels thee in the ways of truth. At all cost obey the Word knowing that My Lord is a rewarder of works and he will render to every man according to his deeds. In other words He'll bless you for blessing one another. Couples who love each other in deed and in truth will face much opposition. For the Godly in Christ shall suffer persecution and as long as couples walk after the spirit, those after the flesh will war against them. Don't let the enemy beguile out of your reward. When two people really love each other in deed and in truth, everything they do adds fuel to the fire and makes their marriage even hotter. Wholesome words and deeds of love are essential for a fruitful and lasting marriage. Love is an unquenchable flame that burns up anything that tries to touch it, harm it, afflict it or smother it. Love is too righteous for the wicked and too strong for the weak.

CHAPTER SEVEN

LIFE OR DEATH

7

LIFE OR DEATH

DEATH AND LIFE ARE IN THE POWER OF THE TONGUE: AND THEY THAT LOVE IT SHALL EAT THE FRUIT THEREOF. (PROVERBS 18:21)

Communication is powerful; it is the sharing and exchanging of thoughts. It is literally the heartbeat of relationships. As with the human body when the heart stops beating that person is pronounced dead. Likewise, when two people stop communicating their relationship is dead. The tongue is powerful because it has the ability to communicate life or to bring forth death. If you want your relationship to flourish the communication must be life-giving. You can't be lying, insulting, cursing, and cutting each other at heart and expect for your relationship not to fall apart.   Life is to be alive, existent, and breathing. Therefore, in order for couples to keep their relationship breathing they must speak life-giving words.

Understand that it's impossible to build or maintain a close relationship with someone you don't talk to. What's the point in being together if you can't have peaceful conversation with them? Men and women should feel at liberty to discuss any and everything with their spouse in the confidence of knowing that their conversation won't be betrayed by them.   They should be able to tell each other their darkest secrets and present issues without the fear of it being thrown in their face or passed through the grape vine. Your spouse should never have to hear what he or she has shared with you in private through another person be it family member or friend. The intimacy you share in communication should be heart to heart.

What often destroys relationships is the lack of communication. It's disheartening for two people to lay beside each other nightly and wake up daily together but yet they can't say more than goodnight and good morning to each other. The less you communicate with anyone the more distant you become with them. Lack of communication is what leads to misunderstanding, arguments, fights, etc. For example, your spouse may not have done many things that you didn't like had you told them in detail what you wanted from him or he beforehand: therefore, to keep down confusion talk to one another. Always express your inner most thoughts with each other, so that you both may learn each other's likes and dislikes.

The Quality of Communication is highly important for a relationship to be fruitful. Your speech should be pure, honest and wholesome words because the way you speak to one another will determine the essence of the time you spend together. If you speak pleasantly to one another, as long as there aren't interferences, you will share a pleasant experience together. A man must cultivate his woman with the Words of God. The Words of God are spirit and they are life. Likewise, a woman must feed her man strength and edify his heart according to the Word of God. A man can't live by bread alone, but by every word that proceedeth out of the mouth of God. The Words of God are bread to the believer and bread strengthens the hearts of men; therefore, couples should absorb and feed each other's spirit by speaking the word of eternal of life to one another. They should strengthen, encourage, and complement one another constantly. Their words should be sweeter than a honeycomb. The Songs of Solomon gives a good example on how couples should speak to and speak of one another. It shows that even in the bedroom there is absolutely nothing wrong with pillow talk. It was sin when you spoke provocative outside of marriage just as sex outside of marriage is a sin, but now that your married you can talk as provocatively as you like to your spouse and it's not a sin.

Couples must watch what come out of their mouths. Profane, vain, or corrupt language should not proceed from their lips.

Many marriages come to a bitter end because of bad communication. When couples lie to one another, scorn, and defame each other their relationship weakens. Divorce shouldn't be spoken of as an option, but once they begin to speak of divorce as a way of escape out of their troubled relationship it becomes an option. Divorce is when a marriage experience death. Death is the end of life. Likewise, divorce is the end of marriage. Life must occur before death can happen; therefore, everything that experiences death, at one point, had to be alive. Examine the things that you are saying and doing that are killing your marriage and refrain from it. Many Marriages have ended due to corrupt communication. When you speak harsh words, lies, and flatter one another, it ruins the relationship. Many relationships would be alive today if the right things had been spoken, but when people prophesy their own destruction they set stage for their demise. When you speak negative things you can expect negative results.

Life and death are like trees that bring forth different types of fruit. The tree of life brings forth the fruits of love, joy, peace, longsuffering, gentleness, meekness, goodness, faith and temperance. The tree of death brings forth the fruits of bitterness, arrogance, hate, sorrow, anxiety, lasciviousness, shame, confusion, etc. for it is **sin.** A person can control what fruits they bear in their own life, by what they speak. For life and death is in the power of the tongue. Therefore, those who love life must speak life and the fruits of life will be manifest in them. Those who love death speak bitter poisonous words and multiply sorrows.

In marriage a wholesome tongue is needed in order for couples to keep their relationship alive, fruitful, and healthy. Couples, who edify one another, speaking life into each other's soul, experience a joyful and peaceful relationship. Love is evident in them because they abide in love. The words they speak to each other fertilize the good fruits that they bear. However, those who

187

bite, devour, curse, and revile each other, bitterness and sorrow rest in their house. For they abide in hell, having a relationship full of discord and malice. Not only when couples curse one another but expressions such as "get out of my life", "I hate you", "I don't want this marriage anymore", "You don't mean nothing to me", "As far as I care, you can go to hell", "Don't touch me", "Don't say nothing to me", "Stay the hell away from me", are a few examples of speaking death. However, those whose marriage continues to press forward, experience life because they are able to talk through their situations and medicate their wounds with healing words.

Couples that are hurting in the area of communication need to pray. If you are speaking the wrong things then change your speech. In order to change your speech, you need to change the meditations of your heart because from the abundance of the heart the mouth speaketh. As children of God we must let our words and the thoughts of our heart be acceptable unto him. Therefore, acknowledge that God hears every word that comes out of your mouth and holds you accountable for them. Don't speak or think anything that you know would displease Him. Speak no lies, nothing profane or vain. Do what you say you're going to do, and don't do what you say you're not going to do because actions speak louder than words. Don't make promises you can't keep. Meaning speak truth always and lie not. Let your conversation be holy and edifying to the hearts of men. Don't think evil, negative, or foolishly. Don't let vain thoughts occupy your mind. When you think on the right things you will begin to speak the right things. In the Word of God it shows us what we should think on.

FINALLY BRETHREN, WHATSOEVER THINGS ARE TRUE, WHATSOEVER THINGS ARE HONEST, WHATSOEVER THINGS ARE JUST, WHATSOEVER THINGS ARE LOVELY, WHATSOEVER THINGS ARE OF A GOOD REPORT; IF THERE BE ANY VIRTUE,

AND IF THERE BE ANY PRAISE, <u>THINK</u> ON THESE THINGS. (PHILLIPIANS 4: 8)

Finally, the Word of God commands that we think positive. The things you think about not only determine the things that come out of your mouth, but it affects your attitude. When you think about good things you will have a good attitude, but if you think about bad reports, bad marriages and situations, you may not believe God for a good marriage. Let your heart meditate on good things. Think about the goodness of God. For one thing is for certain: Jesus is true, honest, just, lovely, praise worthy etc. Therefore, if you can't find anything positive to think about think about the Name of JESUS. There is nothing better or more righteous than He. Don't think about hurting, killing, cursing, cheating, betraying, and divorcing your spouse etc. but think about loving, blessing, touching, building up spouse. Don't think about each other's failures, mistakes, etc. but think about each other's strengths and accomplishments. Uplift and encourage one another.

COMMUNICATIONS

If your relationship is in bad condition somewhere there must be a breach in communication so either

1. It's dishonest communication

2. He or she doesn't know how to talk to you, meaning they take the wrong tone with you when talking to you.

3. Their saying all the "wrong things" aka speaking negatively

4. You're not listening to one Another.

5. You're like Democrats & Republicans you can't agree on anything because you're interpretation and visions of Life are different.

• **Number One:** can be resolved if you follow this scripture:

Ephesians 4:25 Wherefore putting away lying, speak every man truth with his neighbor: for we are members one of another.

• **Number Two:** can be resolved if you apply this scripture:

Proverbs 15:1 A →soft answer← turneth away wrath: but grievous words stir up anger.

• **Number Three:** can be resolved if you apply these scriptures:

Proverbs 8:6-8 Hear; for I will speak of excellent things; and the opening of my lips shall be →right things←For my mouth shall →speak truth← and wickedness is an abomination to my lips. All the words of my mouth are in righteousness;← there is nothing froward or perverse in them.

Remember the power is in your tongue. You must speak life into a sick and dying relationship so that it may be healed because

Proverbs 12:18 There is that speaketh like the piercings of a sword: but the tongue of →the wise is health←

• **Number four:** can be resolved if you apply these scriptures:

James 1:19 Wherefore, my beloved brethren, let every man be swift to hear,← slow to speak,← slow to wrath:←

Proverbs 18:13 He that answereth a matter before he heareth it, it is folly and shame unto him.

• **Number Five:** can be resolved if you Apply this:

Philippians 2:2 Fulfill ye my joy, that ye be likeminded, HAVING THE SAME LOVE, being of one accord, of one mind.

• So that your relationship is balanced make sure you love one another the SAME WAY which is according to the Love of God, so that one won't feel like their giving more than the other one! Come together according to knowledge that you may agree on things. If you do things Gods way you can't go wrong. You must share the same vision because if you two just can't "AGREE" on things, then it's only a matter of time before the relationship utterly falls apart because you're not working together as Teammates, but your fighting one another like opponents.

Amos 3:3 Can two walk together, except they be agreed?

Mark 3:25 And if a house be divided against itself, that house cannot stand.

UNSOLVED MYSTERIES

If your spouse is still bringing up things that happened fromthe first time ya'll met, either he or she hasn't forgiven you OR the issues their bringing up remains an unsolved mystery that they are still trying to solve

1. Although a person can SAY they forgive you for the mistakes you've owned up to, you'll know if they haven't forgiven you from their heart because he or she will harbor bitterness towards you. Inwardly they are still angry with you over it, thus, you'll experience sudden changes in their attitude. Their mood swings will turn day into night and what seemingly appeared to being going as a good and sunny day, will become a dark and raging storm. They'll come out of nowhere and throw your mistakes to your face, thus, spoiling the moment and putting a halt on the rest of the plans you both had made for that day.

2. On the other hand sometimes it not that they didn't forgive you, but if the issues their bringing up wasn't ever resolved, then it is an unsolved mystery and it shall remain an issue until it is solved. If the explanation you gave surrounding the issue doesn't make sense to them, then their still trying to figure out if are you lying to them. He or she may not have proof that you lied, but if your explanation doesn't add up correctly then obviously something isn't right. Until things begin to make sense to them confusion shall remain in the air and they may keep asking you questions periodically as they arise in their mind. Their love for you is what causes them to give you the benefit of the doubt and remain with you, but their love for you doesn't remove the doubts, so the question still remains. What is the truth? Regardless of how much time passes by, they'll always observe and seek to solve the mysteries that are unresolved because in their heart they believe you could be lying about something. So, everything you do that don't appear right will serve as a reminder of everything

you've done that didn't appear right from day one, thus, they may remind you of it because your actions are reminding them of it.

3. The only way to resolve issue that's troubling your relationship is be completely honest with one another. Confessing your faults to another eliminates all confusion. Telling lies to hide your mistakes is like kicking dirt on top of the truth. It may buy you time but eventually the truth will resurface.

Proverbs 12:19, 22

19 The lip of truth shall be established for ever: but a lying tongue is but for a moment.

22 Lying lips are abomination to the LORD: but they that deal truly are his delight.

REASON IT OUT

HE THAT HANDLETH A MATTER WISELY SHALL FIND GOOD: AND WHOSO TRUST IN THE LORD, HAPPY IS HE (Proverbs 16: 20)

Obviously there will be times when husbands and wives won't agree and if it's not handled properly, it could lead to irreconcilable differences. Therefore, pray for wisdom because whenever conflict arise in your relationship it's very important that you deal with it wisely. Always think before you speak and don't be quick to utter every thought that crosses your mind. Many relationships have ended not because of the problem itself, but because of the WAY it was handled. Had they handled the situation God's way something wonderful would have came out of it. However, when you handle a matter foolishly it only creates more problems. Example, a couple gets into an argument over whose turn it is to the buy the dog food, the argument gets heated and the husband gives his wife a tongue lashing. The wife gets mad and decides to stay over at her parent's house for awhile because she feels they need space. A few days pass and the husband decides he will hang out and stay occupied to keep his mind off her. Meanwhile, the wife decides to call up an old male friend of hers to get his opinion. She meets up with her old friend at the coffee shop to chit chat. A friend of her husband's happens to ride pass the place and see her smiling and laughing with another man. He then in-turns calls her husband who becomes furious, jumps in his car, run down to coffee shop and confronts them. He starts accuses her of cheating, causes a big commotion and while she attempts to explain to him, he's not trying to hear nothing she has to say. Him and the other guy gets into a physical altercation leading to one of them getting hurt and the other one getting locked up. The wife feels bad because her innocent friend was wounded and her husband is in jail. Though the argument initiated over dog food, how they handled the situation led to separation, false accusations, injuries, imprisonment, and eventually they were divorced.

DEBATE THY CAUSE WITH THY NEIGHBOR HIMSELF AND DISCOVER NOT A SECRET TO ANOTHER LEST HE HEARETH IT AND PUT THEE TO SHAME, AND THINE INFAMY TURN NOT AWAY. (PROVERBS 25: 9, 10)

At this present moment many are living in regret, feeling responsible for someone's wounds, incarceration, death, etc. due to the fact that they brought outsiders into their domestic dispute. All out family wars have initiated from a minor dispute and its sad to all spilled milk to lead to a blood bath; therefore, to protect others and thyself keep thy mouth closed. Keeping your mouth closed reduces problems because talking too much could put you and/or your spouse in uncomfortable situations. Example, when a man knows his woman is going back feeding her family trash about him, he could feel very uneasy with going over to her relative's house for the holidays. He knows that they don't think too good of him. Therefore, he has to put up with their hypocrisy, watching them smile in his face, knowing if given the opportunity they would hang a rope around his neck. For this cause many men and women stay away from in-law family gatherings. It can feel uncomfortable being around people you know don't like you. You know automatically that everybody in the place is behaving hypocritically by trying to make you feel as though they accept you in their world; however, they really don't want you there. If your spouse would have kept his or her lips sealed about what's been going on in your house, then things would be different.

Sometimes out of anger men and women make hasty decisions such as calling family members, screaming their business over the phone or running over to different people's houses speaking things they should not speak. Married couples never need to complain about their spouse to anyone. Many lie and give others the wrong perceptions of their spouse. Some people talk so bad about their spouse you can't help but ask them, WHY are you still with them? What do they love about your spouse? And you ask them such questions, they cannot give a sufficient answer. For the Word of God says speak evil of no man. Therefore, husbands and wives shouldn't let one negative comment come out of their mouths about each other. Married couples should keep their children out of their disputes as well. They shouldn't want their kids at school explaining in detail to the classroom, how daddy tried to snatch the cell-phone away from momma and cursed her out or how momma was throwing dishes at daddy head after she caught him cheating. Before you know it, you will have social workers knocking at your door and the entire school faculty waiting on a daily report. Understand keeping the doors of your mouth closed prevents a lot of drama from manifesting in your house.

Lastly, Personal things that your spouse has shared about themselves, their family members, friends etc with you is not meant for you to share with anyone else. If it was spoken to you with the expectation that you weren't going to reveal it to anyone else, don't violated that trust. For this very reason many marriages have been ruined. Those things your spouse confides in you about, they shouldn't have to hear about it through the grapevine. You can't deny you said it because if you're the only one they've shared it with, then how did others get knowledge of it? Your spouse should feel comfortable sharing anything with you knowing that whatever he or she speaks to you is in good hands, but when you fumble the ball it causes a communication barrier between you two. If your spouse see that he or she can't tell you anything without you running off at the chops. then they won't tell you anything.

Men, any issue you have with thy wife discuss with her alone. Likewise women, any issue you have thy husband speak with him only. Try your best to resolve the issue without involving anyone else. Many couples make the big mistake of discussing their issues with other people and certain discussions and arguments you have with your spouse shouldn't leave the house. Discussing the problem you have with your mate with someone else certainly won't resolve the problem you have with your mate so why would you walk out the door with them? Sharing your problems with others equip them with the artillery they need to put you to shame. Therefore In order to keep that door of public opinion closed and to keep gossipers from spread rumors and lies rapidly, keep your mouth closed. It's humiliating for you when those you revealed your personal business to in confidence broadcast them to the masses. Everybody at the gym, on your job, at church etc knows your business. When times get heated and thou relationship is getting tried, let it be reemphasized, do not publish it to the world. If you need to say something, tell people to pray for you and your spouse, but don't go running of at the mouth like you have diarrhea and give people detailed accounts about your relationship. Don't turn a private affair into a public forum. Allowing others in your business only opens the door to community involvement, which causes more problems. It could make small matters worse because some things weren't that serious, but when you invited the world into your dispute it will become that serious because the argument grows bigger as more voices entered into it. Thus, the story always seem get twisted and exaggerated, then you find yourself trying to explain the story repeatedly. Your marriage will become the tale of the drunkards and the butt of everyone's joke.

DON'T THROW BOOMERANGS

Bad communication breaks down trust and hardens the heart. Couples that revile one another instead of edifying one another are doomed to fall. Husbands and wives should never disrespect one another and call each other names. Don't allow anger or frustration to lead you to speak curses into your life and marriage.

Be ye ANGRY, and →sin not:← let not the sun go down upon your wrath:(Ephesians 4:26)

Since marriage is a lifelong commitment it will be impossible not to have disagreements. None is perfect, so your spouse will do things rather intentionally or unintentionally that will anger you. Getting angry isn't a sin, but don't allow anger to govern your action and cause you to sin. Don't let your anger lead you to curse them or offend them in any away. Christ himself got angry but he didn't sin against anyone.

And they come to Jerusalem: and JESUS went into the temple, and began →to cast out them that sold and bought in the temple, and overthrew the tables of the moneychangers, and the seats of them that sold doves; (Mark 11:15)

Jesus got enraged when he saw that they turned the House of prayer into a den of thieves. He proceeded to clean house by overthrowing tables and chairs and I have no doubt that He RAISED his Voice at them when he told them to GET OUT. Yet, in doing those things he didn't sin against them. This teaches us regardless of how angry you become even to the point of hitting the wall, tossing tables and chairs, and raising your voice don't lay a finger on your spouse. Example, using the worst case scenario lets imagine a man comes home and find his wife in bed with another man, in this case he has every right to be enraged and its very understandable if he began to flip over tables and chairs, wreck the house, and yell at wife to GET OUT. Yet in spite of how angry he gets he should not sin against her.

At no point nor for any reason should husbands and wives be yelling obscenities and cursing each other out. Good things won't happen to you as long as you are wishing and speaking evil to each other. Many people are catching hell right now because of the things they've spoken over other people's lives. If you want a good life and marriage, certain words should be banned from being spoken from your lips. When you get upset with your spouse do not send her or him to hell with your mouth because your words are like a boomerang returning right back to you. So, in cursing one another you're only cursing yourself so stop throwing boomerangs.

Psalms 109:17 As he loved cursing, so let it come unto him: as he delighted not in blessing, so let it be far from him. 18 As he clothed himself with cursing like as with his garment, so let it come into his bowels like water, and like oil into his bones.

STOP MEDDLING

Know that theirs difference between you trying to talk to your spouse about the concerns on your heart and you trying to get your spouse to talk to you about the concerns on their heart. If you have an issue with the relationship then your spouse doesn't NEED to talk to YOU. The most important thing he or she needs to do is →listen attentively← to you, while you pour out the issues of your heart to them. After you've finishing saying everything you need to say, then give them the opportunity to respond. If they're irresponsive to your concerns don't try to force them to engage in conversation with you. As long as they heard you let them marinate on what you said. If he or she is refusing to listen to anything you have to say, then obviously they either don't care about what you have to say or he or she is intentionally trying to dodge the issues you're bringing to the forefront. If he or she is playing dodge ball that may be your QUE that their guilty of whatever you could be questioning or concerned about. On the contrary, if you're in a situation where your man or woman doesn't want to discuss an issue on their heart, it would be UNWISE of you to try to force him or her to talk to you. Love is patient, so don't press the issue, but let him or her come to you whenever they want to. No need to play →tug-a-war← with the issues on his or her heart. If your spouse isn't ready to talk about it then close your mouth and let it be. If he or she has a stank attitude with you, just leave them be and pray for him or her. Hopefully once he or she is finish smelling themselves, they'll communicate their issues with you, but whatever you do don't keep meddling with it.

Lastly, whenever you do communicate if you see the conversation take a turn for the worse meaning "peace" has forsaken it, then its best to stop feeding into a heated discussion. Once things get steamed, close your mouth, and if need be, leave his or her presence immediately and go cool off somewhere. It wouldn't be WISE to keep talking and meddling with the situation because that may lead to an emergency situation; therefore

It is an honour for a man to cease from strife: but every fool will be meddling. Proverbs 20:3

REMOVE THE BEAM

How you address the issues you have with your spouse is very important. You cannot come at your spouse "twisted," calling yourself trying to straighten him or her out. How do you expect to put anyone in order, if your approach is out of order? Even if it's understandable why your angry and/or correct in what you're saying, you can't come at them in the wrong way expecting to get anything accomplished. Wont anyone receive what you're saying because you don't know how to talk to people. Brothers, you can't call your woman a B*** and think she's going listen to anything that comes out of your mouth afterwards. Sisters, you can't call your man a B**** and think he's going to hear anything you got to say after that either. Don't you dare come at your spouse in the wrong way with the intentions on making it right. You need to flush your own toilet before telling them how to clean theirs.

And why beholdest thou the mote that is in thy brother's eye, but considerest not the beam that is in thine own eye?4 Or how wilt thou say to thy brother, Let me pull out the mote out of thine eye; and, behold, a beam is in thine own eye?5 Thou hypocrite, first cast out the beam out of thine own eye; and then shalt thou see clearly to cast out the mote out of thy brother's eye. (Matthew 7:3-5)

Seriously think about and answer those questions in the scriptures above. Why look at your spouse's imperfection and not acknowledge your own? Why try to put them in order when you're out of order yourself? The first thing you need to do is put an end to your hypocrisy. Acknowledge that neither you nor your spouse are perfect and don't condemn your spouse for his or hers imperfections because in the process of condemning them you're condemning yourself. Example, a man spills something on the carpet or he could be the type of man that is prone to misplacing things. His wife shouldn't blow those things out of proportion nor ridicule him by calling him careless and irresponsible, as though she's never spilled anything or misplaced nothing. We all make mistakes and all mistakes are not necessarily a sin. It's not a sin to accidentally waste something, misplace things, to be late picking someone up, or to leave your underwear on the floor. When your spouse do make mistakes like those it shouldn't cause a fight, so don't be petty and begin to revile or scorn them over it. Understand that throughout life mistakes will be made and unexpected issues are going to occur. However, it solely depends upon how you resolve the issues that will determine the negative or positive impact they have on your marriage. Be quick to listen and get a good understanding of each other by reasoning things out until the situations smoothens out. If the conversation takes a downward spiral and you find yourselves insulting and/or screaming at each other, cease from talking and separate from one another.

BUT IF YE BITE AND DEVOUR ONE ANOTHER, TAKE HEED THAT YE BE NOT CONSUMED ONE OF ANOTHER (Galatians 5: 15)

After you have calmed down and thought things over, resume the conversation at an appropriate time. Neither husband nor wife should have an attitude that they're finish with discussing the issue until both have a clear understanding and have peace about the issue because it will remain an issue until it's resolved. They should never feel it doesn't matter what one or the other thinks, because it does. You should be very concerned with what's going on inside one another other's mind and always pursue and make peace immediately that thy prayers be heard. Do not let the sun go down upon thy wrath.

SILENCE IS GOLDEN

LIKEWISE, YE WIVES, BE IN SUBJECTION TO YOUR OWN HUSBANDS; THAT, IF ANY OBEY NOT THE WORD, THEY ALSO MAY →WITHOUT THE WORD← BE WON BY THE CONVERSATION OF THE WIVES; WHILE THEY BEHOLD YOUR CHASTE CONVERSATION COUPLED WITH FEAR. (1 PETER 3:1, 2)

The mistake many women make is when their husband do step out of line their "methods" of trying to straighten him out is not the way God has ordained for them to do so. The ways of God are peaceful, but many wives take another route that leads to unrest. They'll resort to cursing their husband out, chewing him out, beat him down with scriptures, murmuring and complaining, etc. and none of those methods are effective. If anything they push him further away because the last thing a man want to do is to come home and hear his woman's antagonizing mouth!

When a man begins to fall away from God his woman has the POWER to bring him to his knees before God without speaking one mumbling word! She must learn that Silence is golden. A woman can speak volumes to a man without ever saying a word to him. As hard as it me be for you to do sisters, don't open your mouth, but let your actions speak for you. Understand that the Goodness of God leads you to repentance; therefore, the way a woman influence change in her man, is by letting the Love of God flow through her, that he may experience the goodness of God in her.

Chaste means innocent. Conversation is the Greek word "anastrophe" which means behavior; therefore, it's the way a woman behaves that impacts her man the most. If her behavior is without offense meaning pure, her man can't rightfully accuse of her of being the reason he is acting a fool. He will be forced to take a good look at himself while beholding how good God has been to him, by giving him a woman that's so good to his soul.

The respect and love that a woman gives to her man is the light of God and that light will set that man in order.

Wives, when your husbands are walking disorderly understand your battle isn't with one another, but you're battle is with the Devil. He has waged war against your marriage and your only way to be victories is by an unshakeable faith in Christ. Trust in the Word of My Lord and continue to do right by your husband, though he's not behaving worthy at the time. If he curses you, bless him anyway. If he's getting loud and acting crazy, maintain a quiet spirit. Don't do like many women and start acting a fool as though they're competing for the first place in "The Biggest Dummy Challenge." Don't start club hopping every weekend because he's doing it. Don't stop treating him good just because he's mistreating you. Don't stop praying, reading the Word, and going to Church because he has ceased. Continue to love him anyway and watch how God blesses you in the midst of the storm. As long as he doesn't cross the line, hold on and don't let go. If he does cross the line you have the right to walk out of the marriage. However, if you choose to remain in it, love him till the end. Don't have an affair on him because he has had an affair on you. Don't play the game of tit for tat, though our God is an understanding God, don't allow your husband's misconduct to trigger your disobedience, but overcome the enemy by exercising the Word of God. All a woman must do is stay true to God and If God doesn't repair that man, He will replace that man!

CONFESS YOUR FAULTS

He that covereth his sins shall not prosper: but whoso confesseth and forsaketh them shall have mercy. (Proverbs 28:13)

Many marriages remain in a weak and broken condition because husbands and/or wives won't confess their wrong doings. Confess means to openly acknowledge it and you cannot begin to fix anything, if you don't first acknowledge your part in breaking it. If you know you was wrong, if you know you're guilty of what you're being accused of, If you know you lied, been deceitful, cheated, stepped out of line etc. Come clean about it all. If you keep lying to your spouse telling him or her that you never lied or cheated on them knowing that you have, you are only making matters worse. You might ask God for forgiveness, but it's not enough to tell God that you're sorry for your sins; you need to forsake that sin by confessing the truth to your spouse. It's vain of you to ask for forgiveness for something you haven't repented of. If you're still proclaiming your innocence to them yet confessing your wrong and begging for God's forgiveness, it reveals you fear them more than you fear God.

And fear not them which kill the body, but are not able to kill the soul: but rather fear him which is able to destroy both soul and body in hell. (Matthew 10:28)

Don't fear what they may do if you were to confess the truth to them, but rather fear what God will do to you, if you continue to lie them. If the cost of you confessing the truth and being real before God is losing them, so be it. Don't put their opinions or their feelings above the commandments of God. Yet, this is what many men and women do. They will not confess the Truth because

1. They fear their spouse will leave them.
2. They fear their spouse will harm or seek revenge on them some

kind of way.

3. They don't want to hurt their spouse feelings.

Whatsoever excuse you have for not confessing the truth it's inexcusable. If you fear your spouse will leave if you were to confess the truth, if that be true, then he or she is going to leave you if they ever find out the truth. So as long as you continue to lie to them, you're only keeping them bound to you by deception. The Truth will be exposed, so why deny the inevitable? Get yourself right with God and confess the truth before you're found to be a liar.

If the reason you lie to your spouse is because you feel your spouse has the potential to physically harm or kill you if you were to confess THE TRUTH to them, you may as well RUN away from them now because if they ever find out the TRUTH, you may not know ever know it until that day you come home and meet them sitting in the dark waiting on you. Therefore, get yourself a "safe" distance away from them and once you're completely out of harm's way, then confess the truth to them. Pray and let God lead you to a place of refuge.

Deliver me, O LORD, from the evil man: preserve me from the violent man; (Psalms 140:1)

Understand that it's not love if you're arguing and fighting like cats and dogs, but that is what occurs when you don't see things the same. If your vision and definition of life, marriage, resolving conflict, raising your children and love is completely different from one another, it's like mixing oil and water which simply won't work. Example, if your spouse feel that what you don't know won't hurt you, but you feel what you don't know will hurt you, that's two totally different ways of thinking. So, while you're telling your spouse everything, he or she isn't telling you anything they feel that would upset you; therefore your ways of handling matters are different. While you're disclosing all to them, you'll be wondering why they didn't tell you certain things. Those who believe what you don't know won't hurt you, wont share with you their true medical conditions, sexual orientation, bad habits and addictions, eetc This is why many marriages are suffering and some ended immediately because many women and men didn't find out the truth about their spouse until they married their spouse. It wasn't until they said "I DO" that they discovered WHO they really got married to. It was made known to them some kind of way that their spouse was disease ridden, down low, drug addict, violent, gambling habit, etc. Yet had they been honest in the beginning about who they were a lot of pain, embarrassment, and misery would have been avoided and although he or she said they love you, it wasn't love at all. Spare one another the drama and always be honest with one another because the Word says in order to be made whole you must

Confess your faults one to another, and pray one for another, that ye may be healed. The effectual fervent prayer of a righteous man availeth much. (James 5:16)

- **HUMBLE YOURSELF**
- **PRAY** without ceasing (Believe that prayer changes things)
- **ASK** Others To Pray for you
- **ANOINT** Yourself With Holy Oil (Pure Olive Oil daily)
- **CONFESS YOUR FAULTS** Don't hide but acknowledge your mistakes. Speak the truth to all those you've lied to!
- **BE MERCIFUL.** If you want GOD to have Mercy on you then have Mercy on others and be a blessing all people in your life.
- **HAVE FAITH** because without faith it's impossible to please Him. You must do the will of God and believe He will do whatever it is your asking of Him without wavering.

If my people, which are called by my name, shall humble themselves, and pray, and seek my face, and turn from their wicked ways; then will I hear from heaven, and will forgive their sin, ←and→will heal their land. (2 Chronicles 7:14)

CHAPTER EIGHT

BUILT TO LAST

8

BUILT TO LAST

Except the LORD build the house, they labour in vain that build it: except the LORD keep the city, the watchman waketh but in vain. (Psalms 127:1)

What is your marriage founded upon? Are you a match-made in heaven or a match made in hell? Examine yourself, are you doing things God's way? It's vain for couples to work day and night at trying to get their marriage to function right if they have excluded God out of it, because when you exclude God out of your marriage Love is nowhere to be found in it.   Many relationships that started off wonderfully have ended up disastrous because God wasn't the founder and architect of it. As He gave Noah very detailed instructions on how to build a boat strong enough to endure a FLOOD that was coming to destroy all the inhabitants of the earth, He also give us specific instructions on how to build relationships strong enough to stand the storms that are coming to destroy everything in its path. Had Noah not hearkened to the voice of God humanity would not have been saved but by faith Noah made an Ark and was prepared for the storm. Are you prepared for what lies ahead? If you don't follow the blueprint you nor your relationship will stand the storm. Don't be distracted by what the rest of the world is doing. If your living by faith you'll see what the rest of the world doesn't see and if you don't hearken to the voice of the Lord your marriage is guaranteed to fall apart from the storm. However, if you let Christ the master builder and wise counselor be your guide, he will lead you in the way of peace. His Word is the roadmap to having a fruitful and lasting marriage to them who are faithful and patient in spirit. One thing is for certain, if thy house is built upon the Rock nothing that comes against it will be able to shake it.

Therefore whosoever heareth these sayings of mine, and doeth them, I will liken him unto a wise man, which built his house upon A Rock:25 And the rain descended, and the floods came, and the winds blew, and beat upon that house; and it fell not: for it was founded upon a rock.(Matthew 7:24-25)

Hearken to the Word of God because the durability of your marriage is determined by its foundation. The Lord engineered the storms that shall try your marriage, so He's knows the materials and the tools and time needed in order for you to build a durable relationship. It is pertinent for couples that want to survive the storms to be doers of the Word of Truth. His Love is the only element strong enough to any and every kind of trial life can throw at you. You can't love your spouse the way you want to love him or her. You can't orchestrate your marriage the way you want and expect for it to stand. It may start off great, but over time it will begin to crack under pressure; therefore, give your ear to the Word of the Lord and implement exactly what he tells you to do because everything God builds is built to last. Submit to God and structure your relationship according to His design. If your hearers of the word only, you're only deceiving yourselves and the wreckage made from the storm will expose that. If you hearken to the Voice of God no matter which way the enemy comes at you nothing will move you. You may not understand some of the things that God direct you to do, but trust in the Lord at all times and don't deviate from His instructions.

The most important part in building a house is the Foundation. If the foundation isn't strong it doesn't matter how big or expensive the house is, it will collapse when the winds of adversity blows against it. The Rock which is the Word of God is the only substance strong enough to stand the turbulence; therefore, don't subscribe to any doctrine that contradicts or perverts the Gospel of Jesus Christ. Married couples should not seek worldly council. Stop hearkening to books, videos, or anybody that gives you guidance contrary to his Word. The reason why many marriages are weak and fruitless is because they follow man's doctrine of love and marriage instead of God's doctrine, thus, they are merely wasting their time.

And every one that heareth these sayings of mine, and doeth them not, shall be likened unto a foolish man, which built his house upon the sand:27 And the rain descended, and the floods came, and the winds blew, and beat upon that house; and it fell: and great was the fall of it.(Matthew 7:26-27)

When you don't obey God your standing on shaky ground. Your marriage will not endure temptations because you have founded it upon a false hope. Many couples go to Church and pray all the daylong, but yet and still, their relationship ends in divorce or it's fruitless because they never turned from their wicked ways and obeyed the Lord. Example, some of them foolishly believed in that old saying that says, "a family that prays together stays together" and this is far from the truth. Prayer alone won't keep your marriage together because if you're **praying** together, but not **obeying** Him, your prayers are not being heard. The face of My Lord is against those that doeth evil, therefore, it's wiser to say, "When two people pray and obey the Lord they shall stay as one." Because

TO OBEY IS BETTER THAN SACRIFICE. (1 SAMUEL 15:22)

Instead of obeying God the children of Israel would rather disobey his commands and give the Lord a sacrifice for their sin but God finds no delight in those who won't hearken to Him. Therefore, don't try to flatter God with words but obey him. You don't impress Him by going to Church, paying your tithes and doing the Holy Ghost dance acting as though you're holier than thou. Telling Him how wonderful, awesome and powerful He is, but yet you won't humble yourself under His mighty hand is like playing games with him. Take heed to your spirit, God is not playing any games with you. Obey him and cease from doing

211

things your way, although you may like it your way understand your way is VAIN. Example, your way could be to sleep in different rooms but God wants you to sleep together, your way could be to go days without speaking before you forgive one another, but God wants you to forgive from your heart immediately and to not let the sun go down upon your wrath understanding that tomorrow is not promised. Your way could be to resolve your issues violently, but God want you to resolve things peacefully. Your way could be a "swingers" marriage, but God wants you to have a "monogamous" marriage. Your way may be to let the wife take the lead in the house, but God wants the husband to be head of the house. Your way may be to render evil for evil, but God want you to render good for evil! Your way may be to lie and manipulate your spouse to do the things you want, but God wants you to be Honest and honor one another. When you do things his way no weapon formed against your marriage will prosper.

ONE OF A KIND

As the lily among thorns, so is my love among the daughters. As the apple tree among the trees of the wood, so is my beloved among the sons. I sat down under his shadow with great delight, and his fruit was sweet to my taste. (Song of Solomon 2:2-3)

When husbands and wives walk in the Love of Christ the love they give to one another should be uniquely different and better than the love they receive and give to everyone else. A man or woman shouldn't be making their spouse feel as though they received or receive a better love elsewhere. If a man loves his wife the way Christ loves his Church what other man can love her better than he can. Likewise, If a woman is submitting to her husband in everything as the word teaches her to. If she is woman of a meek and quiet spirit what other woman can love her husband better than she can. This is why it's important for Husbands and wives to hearken to the doctrines of Christ, so that their marriage can be a true reflection of love. The way they'll love an honor one another will be different from those of the world. Their style, their speech, their way of thinking, and their personality will be one of a kind because God has fearfully and wonderfully made them. Their love for thee is sweeter than others. They'll touch your heart and soul in ways that it has never been touched. Their distinguished and the things they do and are willing to do for thee, others are too proud to perform.

As a woman the way you love your man should be like none other. That love should be so good to him that he can't compare it to any other woman he knows from his past or present. The honor and respect you give to him should supersede what others give him. He should be able to look into your eyes and say he never experienced a love like yours. The things you do for him others may call you a fool for doing it, but that is what set you apart from them. Your love is as a Lilly among thorns to him. Likewise Husbands, if you love your woman the way God commanded you to, which is the way Christ so loved his Church there is no greater love than that. You should love all people, but the love you give to her should be without measure. NO other man should move her soul the way you do. NO other man should be there for her more than you. You held on to her while all others let go. She should find it a joy just to be in your presence because there's something so different and special about you, that she can't keep her hands and lips off you. Your love should make her crave all of you all the time because if you love her the way Heaven requires you to, that love will be one of a Kind.

Example, the love of God will wash your feet; his love is thoughtful of you and gives good gifts without repentance unto you just because. It will open any door for you. It will nurse you when you're sick. It will encourage you when you're down. It won't just drop you off at the hospital, but it stands by your side and waits with you at the hospital. It will long-suffers with you as you grow. It won't speak foolishly to you, but it feeds you knowledge and understanding. It won't lie to you, but on the contrary it's brutally honest with you. It accompanies you where ever you want it to go with you. It prays for you unceasingly. It confesses it faults and tries to correct its mistakes. It always forgives you, a man or woman of God always forgives. It helps you carry your burdens and make you feel like a blessing. It believes in and supports your dream. In essence, others might have showed a little love, but men and women of God show God's love which surpasses human understanding. It stays with you while others fall away from you. It's a sanctified love that you won't find in carnal minded men. Many claimed to have loved you and they could have really felt in their heart that they loved you, but if their love hurt you, it's because their love wasn't the Love of God.

King Solomon found this type of love in one of his wives. For her love for him couldn't be categorized with other women who had claimed to have loved him. She didn't love Solomon because of his position or for his money. She didn't love his apron but she loved the things that were in him. She loved his Spirit and his wisdom. She loved his heart and his voice. She loved his faith, his character, his strength and his beauty. She cherished his soul. For she would do things for him that others never would've thought of doing. Many women didn't have the courage to do the things she did. They spoke evil of her, calling her a fool for her man because she was willing to forsake all to be with him. She was as a sheep in the midst of ravenous wolves.. She was the talk of the town. Lies, jealousy, and envy spoke harsh words against her because they hated the way she loved.

Has someone ever called you foolish for supposedly loving your spouse too much? Has a person scorned thy name because thou went through or was willing to go through extremes to be with your heart's desire? Never think you're a fool for loving your spouse too much. If you love your spouse the way Christ loved the Church, the devil will say that's too much love, and call you a fool. However, you're a fool for Christ and your spouse will be a fool if he or she ever walks away from that love. Many of the Apostles were called fools for Christ because not only did they give up all things for Him, they suffered greatly for His name sake. If you ever meet someone who loves thee in a way that they're willing to pay whatever price they have to pay to abide with thee, whether it cost the forsaking of family, friends, lands, along with persecutions and suffering for the Lord's sake to be with you, thou have met a person who cherishes and values the will of God and that bears their cross. He or she won't let thee go regardless of how strong the winds blow. It's that kind of love husbands and wives should always have for one another. The only thing that is more valuable than the relationship between them, is their relationship with Christ. However, if they value their relationship with Christ they will never stop loving each other the same way Christ loves the Church because that's God's will. They should find great peace and pleasure in each other's presence. Their love should be as a precious genuine gem in the midst of counterfeits. They should cleave unto each other and never detach themselves from one another. Their love for one another should flow naturally like rivers of water permeating through the streets. Love moisturizes all dry areas of life. There aren't any defects in the love of Christ. All that witness it, can't believe their eyes and all that experience it, are blessed above measure. It's a love that is too intense for shallow people. It's a perpetual love that provokes many to jealousy. True love and friendship is never to be taken for granted. It's good for the soul. For many want it but won't pay the price it takes to have it, but you lay hold of it and do not let it go. Love is one of the good fruits of the Spirit. The righteous must bear good fruits in order to be Glorified and couples who don't bear good fruit will not love each other, nor will they experience joyful times or peace with one another. Satan's main concern is that you bring forth evil (or no fruit) to production, because every branch that abides in Christ that brings not forth good fruit, He shall cast away and gather them for the flames. It's important to always love one another so that your fruit may multiply in times of the harvest, never to wither away. That's when God the Father is glorified in you and your relationship.

Jesus, like none other, was crucified and died on the cross. There is no greater love than this, to lay down his life for friends. In return, the first commandment is that we love Him with all our heart, mind, soul, and strength. For there isn't any greater or better love than the Love of Christ. His love is patient, kind, not self-seeking, not rude nor proud. It hopeth, believeth, endureth, and beareth all things. It rejoices not in evil but with the truth. It keeps no record of evil. Whenever thou locate that type of love, don't lose it. Thou have found something more precious than anything this world can ever offer.

WORK TOGETHER

TWO ARE BETTER THAN ONE; BECAUSE THEY HAVE A GOOD REWARD FOR THEIR LABOUR BUT WOE TO HIM THAT IS ALONE WHEN HE FALLETH, FOR HE HATH NOT ANOTHER TO HELP HIM UP. (Ecclesiastes 4:9)

Sometimes the question is raised, "Is it better to be single or married?" However, according to the scriptures above when you're married it's never a question of were you better off remaining single, unless your companion is a devil {fool} because one of the beauties of Marriage is that you are never alone. God has provided you with all the help you need in the one he has joined you to. You're each other's keeper. Your spouse is your lifetime companion and co-laborer under the sun. This is why it's important for couples to be on one accord because when they labor TOGETHER as one, much progress is made being that they are working WITH one another and not against each other. Understand marriage is a joint-effort. Husbands and wives must look at themselves as team-mates because in order to build a lasting and fruitful marriage it requires TEAMWORK!

Definition of teamwork: cooperative or coordinated effort on the part of a group of persons acting together as a team or in the interests of a common cause.

The man and his woman can only birth the vision that God has given them of Marriage, when they both agree on the vision and work together according to His Will. They each have a position to fulfill, so it's important that they know their job description and carry out the duties demanded of it. As long as they walk with God, He will recompense all the works of their hands. Many Marriages don't last because too many husbands and wives are disingenuous. If you want your relationship to work let not your love be counterfeit. Couples that are not real with one another are not only fooling themselves, but they are a huge stumbling block to others as well. Their marriage is toxic because it poisons the desire that others could have to be married. Many people this day refuse to ever get married because they witnessed the corruption in the marriages of those around them. Some took that stance when they learn that "the couple" they thought would never break up suddenly ends in divorce. These are the couples that indeed appeared beautiful outwardly unto men by putting on Oscar worthy performances. Whenever their seen together in public places such as church, the gym, malls, family gatherings and social events, etc. their holding hands and displaying public affection. However, from the outside looking in, they look like the perfect couple and unless you had an eye on the inside of their house you never would have known that HELL resided there. They have on masks and read scripts for their audience, but as soon as the stage lights goes off and the curtains drop, they take off their costumes and cease from speaking their Romeo and Juliet lines to one another. Their public joy ends when they walk inside they're hell-hole, so the smile people see on their faces is only there to hide the misery in their heart. This should not be the case. God want his people to be genuine and exhibit real love inside and outside their home. If you truly love one another, that love will be seen publicly, but even more so privately because your love can get naked when your alone. Genuine love doesn't change faces when the lights are on or when the lights are off. It is constant in and out of the spotlight.

A GEM

- a cut and polished precious stone or pearl fine enough for use in jewelry.
- something likened to or prized as such a stone because of its beauty or worth:
- a person held in great esteem or affection.
- Brit. Printing . a 4-point type of a size between brilliant and diamond.

Its amazing how the true character of those in your circle are exposed when you start going through challenging situations. You find out in the storm that many of your loved ones and friends are not genuine because when the rain came in your life, they ran out your life. So be sure to acknowledge and give great respect to all those who have endured your storm because in doing so, they proved their loyalty to you. That person that stood in the rain and stayed soaking wet with you until the sun started shining again in your world is a GEM. A GEM is a cut and polished precious stone and it's rare to find. It's been found in some of the oddest places, but regardless of where you find ONE even if you find it in someone else's garbage, you better hold on to it and Thank God for it. It may not be perfect, but gems are very valuable even with their flaws. They bring brilliance and a radiance glow into your life. If you offend them in any way you got to answer to God. Some are going through storms right now because they offended the one that Heaven sent to them.

Husbands and wives need to be one another Gem and see one another as each other's Gem. Once you see your spouse as your gem, you won't do anything that jeopardizes losing her or him. You won't put yourself in any position to lose them because you both understand there is nothing under the sun more valuable in life than one another. When one of you falls, the other is there to support and help them through all of their darkest moments. Understand, It's a blessing to have someone who show themselves to be true to you through better and for worse, through sickness and in health, through richer and poorer, loving you till death do you part. Don't take your spouse for granted. You're so much stronger with her or him. When two stand as one in agreement with God, He promises that it won't be easy for the enemy to break that threefold cord. Truly understand to have a friend that loves you at all times and supports you in all ways is a blessing from God, and if thou art married that friend should be your spouse. Husbands and wives take care of your Gem before you find your Gem in some else's possessions wishing you had not lost it. GOD saw the sacrifices they made and the loyalty they gave to you and they shall reap what they've sown. If you don't give them the same love they gave you, God is going bless them with the love that you wouldn't give them and so much more.

TUG OF WAR

- Is defined as an athletic contest between two teams at opposite ends of a rope, each team trying to drag the other over a line.

- a hard-fought, critical struggle for supremacy.

In marriage your spouse should be your teammate not your opponent, but if the latter be your situation instead of your marriage being a joint venture, it will feel like a tug of war. You can't have peace nor will you ever learn to trust someone that's constantly pulling against you. If every time you say yes, your spouse says no, you say left and they say right, you say north and they say south, if every time you debate with anyone and your spouse joins forces with those opposing you, it reveals that their heart is against you. Your marriage shouldn't be a hard fought struggle against each other. A man shouldn't have to pull and drag his wife along with him. Husband and wives must know their place and stop fighting one another for supremacy. Be supportive of each other's dreams and stop behaving as though you're racing against one another. Don't attempt to sabotage your spouse's plans just so your plan can stand. God cannot bless your relationship if all you two do is war against each other, therefore, stop trying to outdo one another, but beautify each other knowing when one looks good the other looks good, when one succeed, you both succeed. Encourage one another to be the best that they can be and applaud one another's accomplishments. You should love to see each other look good, smell good, feel good, and prosper in all that you both has set out to do. A wife should be her husband's number one cheerleader, and a man should be his woman's biggest fan.

If you can't stand together you won't be together long because eventually a divided house must come to end. If you want your marriage to survive you must get on the same page and stop challenging one another. Stop trying to sabotage each other's dream. Encourage and push one another into the sea of success instead of pulling each other into the quicksand of failure. God will not bless your marriage until you get to the place of understanding that you are no more twain, but ONE and behave as One. When people can behold the beauty of your marriage, that's when God shall let his dew fall upon it.

Behold, how good and how pleasant it is for brethren to dwell together in UNITY! It is like the precious ointment upon the head, that ran down upon the beard, even Aaron's beard: that went down to the skirts of his garments, as dew of Hermon, as the dew that descended upon the mountains of Zion: for THERE the Lord commanded the blessing, even life evermore(Psalms 133)

In Conclusion, when people get married they have vowed to be on the same side (team). Therefore, they should be best friends and partners. When you're teammates you should never oppose one another, but work together to overcome any obstacle that standing in your way of being victorious. One shouldn't try to outshine or outdo the other one. You are co-laborers of love completing the task that God has laid before you. Everything that you can do as a couple to sharpen, enhance, and enrich your marriage that's of truth, you should submit to.

GET NAKED

AND THEY WERE BOTH NAKED THE MAN AND HIS WIFE AND THEY WERE NOT ASHAMED. (GENESIS 2:25)

When God made Adam and Eve he made them both naked and they weren't ashamed, meaning there wasn't any area of their lives that was hidden from each other nor was there anything about their lives that they were ashamed of. They didn't have any skeletons in the closet. Adam knew everything about Eve. Likewise, Eve knew every little detail about Adam. Nothing was hidden from each other's eyes; therefore, their hearts were secure in one another. They didn't have to figure out what they were hiding or keeping from each other because they had no secrets. They didn't wonder why this? Or, why that? They didn't play those mind games with each other because they kept it real with one another by being completely exposed and not ashamed of anything. They didn't have any such thing as PRIVACY RIGHTS between them

As Adam and Eve, husbands and wives should have access to every part of each other's life. They should know all things about one another because when you're married, you are one. As one, there is no such thing as having your own life or personal space. Therefore, a man or woman should never make their spouse feel as though he or she is invading there space or crowding their territory. If you have nothing to hide, there's no need to deny your spouse entry to any part of thy life, nor should you catch an attitude with thy spouse when he/she feels the need to search things out. There shouldn't be any problem for couples to have access to each other's cell phone, emails, face-book, purse, and wallet, lock box, etc. Whenever a man or woman doesn't want their spouse to answer their phone, listen to their voicemail, read their emails and inbox messages, go through any of their "belongings," or know certain things about their past, that's enough to raise their eyebrow and cause them to question, "Why not? What is there to hide? What dark secret are you trying to keep covered?" Some men and women are unaware that their spouse even owns second cell phone or have profile pages on other social sites. If you care about your spouse, you would secure their heart and one way of doing that is to not make it appear as though you're hiding something from them because regardless if you get naked voluntary or not, what's in the dark always comes to light.

If it takes your spouse to look through your items everyday to establish trust between you two, there shouldn't be any problem with that, especially if you've sown mistrust into the relationship. Not that he/she should or would go through your belongings daily, but they should never be denied the right to do so. If you show that you have an issue with them going through it, that alone appears you have something you don't want them to see.   Every devil in hell says, "Why can't or don't you trust me?" Or they scream that they don't have to prove themselves to you because they have no reason to lie. Action speaks louder than words, a person can always debate what you say, but once you prove it to them, they can't say anything. Therefore, if you love someone why wouldn't you give them proof? If giving the proof clears their conscious, and strengthens their trust, you should diligently do so and bring peace to the heart of the one you say you love. Whenever it's in your power you should always clean up the mess you made and whatever mistake you make that can't be corrected by you, pray to God and let Him clear up the confusion for you. If things don't appear right, then understand that man judges by outward appearance. With all the game playing, lies, and hypocrisies in this sin sick world, you should understand why a person would want to search things out and be sure that the person that their giving their heart to isn't deceiving them. Many people are living double lives and are deceitful in their ways.

Therefore, it's only wise of a person to observe and analyze everything, so do your part in making it easy for them to, by providing what's necessary to establish trust between you two.

Understand, when God made Adam and Eve naked; He never wanted a man or his wife to have anything to hide from each other. Too many people have never gotten completely naked with their spouse. Getting naked requires you to expose everything about yourself to your spouse. Don't withhold pertinent information from you spouse or lie to conceal hatred. You can't have true peace until you have spoken the truth. People lie because they fear the consequences of speaking the truth. Though speaking the truth could have many people running out of your life, if that is what it costs to be real and to be in right standing with God, then pay the price. God delights in those who deal truly and he shall bless you for being real. It's far better for you to tell your spouse the truth or eventually the Holy Spirit will do it for you. The Holy Spirit will expose you. If you deny the truth, after the truth has been revealed, thinking that lying might save or spare your relationship from turmoil, it doesn't. However, the lie (sin) brings the relationship into bondage stunting the growth and damages it more so in the long run. For confusion always follows lies. Sin of any sort leads us down the road of reproach, shame, and dishonor. However, healing can take place after confessions and prayers are made. Don't think lying will band aid the wound. Lies can be like walking time bombs that come nicely gift wrapped. It might sound good and produce a false peace for the moment, but it's only a matter of time before it blows up in thy face.

FOR I ACKNOWLEDGE MY TRANSGRESSIONS: AND MY SIN IS EVER BEFORE ME. (PSALM 51:3)

Many marriages are not lasting because too many are too prideful to acknowledge they're wrong, and apologize for it. Their pride is going to lead them straight into hell. They'd rather walk away from the relationship and let it die before they ever confess the truth. Many will have the audacity to insult your character when you confront them about their mistake. They'll call you stupid, ignorant, foolish, and a liar, while inwardly knowing that you have spoken nothing but the truth concerning them.

Some will deny or tell a little truth to get you to believe the big lie. He will try to make you think that you don't know what you are talking about when it's obvious he is full of it. A fool would rather hide his sin instead of confessing the truth and keeping it real because regardless to what we do to cover ourselves, the fig leaves won't work. It takes My Lord to cover our nakedness, for He had clothed Adam and Eve with coats of skin and as of this day He promises to clothe those who believe in His name, in white garments. However we can't be forgiven until confession is made. Therefore, confess your fault one to another, ask them to forgive you, then pray and ask God to forgive you, and if people don't forgive you, forgive yourself and let it go. Since God has forgiven us, He commands we forgive one another and hold no grudges. For forgiveness is in the heart of the believer. Therefore, couples must be patient, pray and be willing to forgive.

Another very important reason why Husbands and wives shouldn't withhold anything about themselves from one another, is because your enemies always dig up mess about you and use it against you. Satan will reach far back into your history and try to find something you buried long ago to cause confusion between you and the one you love. Yet, if you already know everything there is to know about your spouse, there is nothing the adversaries can inform you that will take you by surprise. The only thing left for your enemies to do is do what they do best, which is lie. However, if you're not aware of everything concerning your spouse and someone tells you something about your spouse that you didn't know, especially when you thought you knew everything, it hurts. It could deeply wound the wall of trust in the relationship and possibly destroy your marriage; therefore, getting naked with one another is protecting your marriage. Every marriage will be tried by fire, and one of Satan's methods is to dig up all the shameful mess in your life, in hopes of changing your spouse's perception and feelings towards you.

AN UNGODLY MAN DIGGETH UP EVIL. (PROVERBS 16:28)

Only ungodly people won't let your past go. They'll dig up and dangle your grade school mistakes over your head. They won't believe you've grown since elementary or that you've been transformed into a new creature in Christ. Though the past is behind you, any information that they feel they can use to steal your joy and to destroy your life, they will search out and season it by adding lies to it. If you truly want to fortify your marriage, If there's any secrets that a man or woman has not shared with their spouse, it should be discussed. It could greatly damage your relationship if it is exposed through a different source. For the adversaries do everything they can to change the minds of those who honor you. For example, in a courtroom when an attorney wants to discredit an eye witness testimony, they'll shovel up every amount of dirt they can use to defame that person's character. They'll paint a dark picture of him/her because under no circumstance do they want the jury to believe the witness' account. This same method is used by Satan when he afflicts a marriage. He digs up as much information as he can on the husband and/or wife that could be used to sow distrust and divide them. Relationships that are weak and not founded upon the Rock will eventually fall. If the truth has been established beforehand, then there is nothing that the ungodly can say or uncover that can move a husband and wife against each other.

A HYPOCRITE WITH HIS MOUTH DESTROYETH HIS NEIGHBOR: BUT THROUGH KNOWLEDGE SHALL THE JUST BE DELIVERED. (PROVERBS 11:9)

You'll be surprised who t he enemy will use to try to poison your marriage. Some of you're so called "close" relatives and friends that are smiling in your face will be the one's saying damaging things about you and by them being near to you, it will make what they say more believable. However, the more truth that you know will set your marriage free from the entanglement of the enemy. If you're living right by God and standing on his Word, the Lord promises you deliverance. The enemy won't succeed in poisoning your relationship by digging up thy past secrets and sins. Through knowledge marriages are liberated and can grow unceasingly because how can the enemy defeat you However, many marriages are abound in afflictions because of their ignorance of truth. They perish because of the lack of knowledge. Though some marriages might last a long time many of them are unfruitful being full of sorrows. When couples are ignorant to how their enemies operate they don't know how to stand against them. Satan always attempts to break down the wall of trust and intimacy in relationships. Trust is essential to having a fruitful and lasting marriage. However, when a husband or wife doesn't trust each other, it becomes a constant struggle for them to remain together. They will question each other's every move. They wouldn't listen to or honor one another's words. For it's sad to have to say that you know that your spouse is a habitual liar. It's a shame when you can't trust a word that comes out of their mouth or when anyone knows something about thy spouse that you don't know. Therefore, always be honest, talk to one another and share those things that are uncomfortable for you to speak about. If that person is of My Lord and walks in love they shall rejoice in knowing the truth. It might be uneasy at first. However, once digested it shall make the bond stronger. Lying in any shape, form, or fashion is a sin and always keep in mind that sin weakens thee. Therefore, lying to one another for any reason weakens the relationship. When the adversaries shoot their arrows, the chances of enduring or passing the test is highly unlikely if thou relationship is established upon lies. Once lies enter into a relationship the relationship goes into captivity, it can't grow in truth nor bring forth good fruits of the spirit.

THE LIP OF TRUTH SHALL BE ESTABLISHED FOREVER: BUT A LYING TONGUE IS BUT FOR A MOMENT. (PROVERBS 12:19)

Lies don't exist long because it's only a short matter of time before truth is exposed. The truth liberates you from whatever had you bound by deception. Lies held you captive in a dark place but the truth sets you free. Lying is an act of hate but Truth is an act o love: therefore, always speak the truth regardless to how much it might hurt the one you love, because the mouth of truth is established forever. Truth is the life of a good relationship. Husband and wives should make one another feel comfortable enough to sharing anything with each other because lies are often told when someone fears your reaction to the truth. However, when your totally honest with one another, there's nothing the enemy can catch you by surprise you with. Example, out of envy your spouse's sibling or friend may tell you something personal about your spouse that they thought you didn't know and hand you not known it could have infuriated you, but when you already know it shuts the enemy down. You should praise My Lord because the weapon they (the enemy) used with the intent of destroying your marriage backfired. Seeing that they envy your marriage and could not succeed in breaking it up, should bring you and your spouse closer together, and strengthen your faith in the Word of God. The enemy extremely hate couples that let the Word dwell in them richly because he can't conquer them. However when you don't know everything about your spouse and the enemy catches you off guard it could ruin your marriage. For example, let's assume a woman prior to knowing her husband made sex-tapes with her ex-boyfriend that she never told her husband about, and one day her ex-boyfriend post the video in one of those face-book groups that a sibling of her husband belong to, who in turns shows it to her husband. Although the videotapes took place before she knew her husband, if she never told him about them, it could cause all hell to break loose in their relationship. If they already have trust issues in their marriage, that could be the icing on the cake or if she looks the same way she looks in the video, her husband may not be able to tell when the tapes were produced. It's highly important for couples to discuss the dirt in each other's life preferable before marriage, to avoid the snares of the wicked. The enemy won't have anything to dig up if it's already known. Some people waited till after they got married to come clean about certain things in their past believing that it wouldn't matter, but it did and has led some couples to divorce. You don't want your spouse to feel as though he or she has been deceived by you and/or to regret that they married you. To avoid such traps, talk to one another, speak the truth in love that one another may be prepared for the unexpected.

Though at one point we were clothed in shame, if we surrender all to My Lord, he will in turn clothe us with glory, honor, wisdom, and righteousness that the nakedness of our shame does not appear, and make us white in the blood of the Lamb. Before we can be clothed and wrapped in glory, we must first take off the aprons, be strip down to the core of our souls, and look at ourselves for who we really are. We must accept our past, our problems, and confess our mistakes, understanding that we are not without sin. We can no longer hide behind leaves. We must throw away the costumes and be real. Only until we are honest with ourselves and with others, can My Lord cover and heal us. You must lay everything on the altar, stop trying to dress yourself and let the Love of God embrace thee, heal thy wounds, and wash thy sins away.

LOVE ME NAKED

When My Lord created Adam and Eve, he made them pure in heart. They didn't have the knowledge of evil. Therefore, they didn't know how to disrespect one another. They couldn't batter, abuse, or revile each other, because evil had no part in them. All they knew was My Lord, for He is Love. Therefore, all they knew how to do was love one another. Their ways were of love and they rested in the presence of God experiencing the fullness of joy. They were happy together. They were naked and bare, being totally exposed and having only love to give to one another. They couldn't impress one another with material things such as clothes, cars, houses, jewelry, or anything that money could buy, but their innate qualities had a deep impact on each other. They couldn't love the things that thou can posses and lose. They had to love one another for who they really were. They had to love each other's mind, body, soul and spirit. They loved each other's character and attitude. They loved each other's presence. They couldn't war over material things but they shared all they had, which was their thoughts, their heart, their bodies, and they weren't ashamed.

...AND THE EYES OF BOTH OF THEM WERE OPENED, AND THEY KNEW THEY WERE NAKED; THEY SEWED FIG LEAVES TOGETHER AND MADE THEMSELVES <u>APRONS</u>. (GENESIS 3:7)

After sin entered the world, the first thing that came into existence was clothes (apron). Adam and Eve made aprons to cover themselves. Today, people still wear aprons. The apron would be considered the external attributes of a person and/or material things. The apron consists of a person's wardrobe, car, house, job, money, education, etc. Many people hide behind aprons and some use their aprons as bait to catch you in their trap because many make the mistake of judging a person's worth according to the apron. The apron doesn't determine a person's nature, it doesn't define a person's character, nor does it reveals the intent and motives of someone's heart. The apron doesn't make you honest, stronger, or wiser. The apron is actually worthless. However, the apron can deceive those who are driven by lust. Those who put their trust in their apron can become prideful or arrogant because they think their apron is better than others, while others have low self-esteem because they don't like the apron they're wearing. The apron does not reflect who you are, nor can it make you any better than what you are. Many have married someone because of the apron he or she was wearing and found themselves bound to a fool. They married an individual for his or her money, title, possessions and bragged of those things to others. However, if a person only speaks of the apron someone is wearing and never emphasizes how wise, peaceful, loving, gentle, giving, kind, and beautiful someone's spirit is, then he or she values the wrong thing. Many walk around in sheep's clothing, but inwardly their ravenous wolves; therefore, if you only speak of the apron your spouse is wearing, the question remain are you married to a wolf or a sheep?

Many men and women have walked away from their marriage once their spouse took off their apron. The apron was the only thing that kept them holding on so once the Apron came off the truth was in plain sight and they didn't see anything worth hanging on to. They could not accept the truth about their spouse, and the reality is many people cannot handle the truth this is why they find fig leaves to hide behind. When a person loves your apron more than your presence (spirit), if anything happens to your apron they'll walk away from you Godspeed. However, if they value your presence in their life than, regardless of the apron that you're wearing they don't want to lose you. They could not accept the truth, and the reality is many people cannot handle the truth. It's foolish for anybody to value aprons. An apron can't walk with you, talk with you, eat with you, or sleep with you. An apron can't love you, hold you, or cultivate you. An apron can't do nothing more than give you a certain appearance. If you can't love people when their aprons are off and their nakedness is exposed, then you don't love them. If you don't love them when they have nothing but themselves to give, then you don't love them. If you don't love their spirit, attitude, and character, and value their presence in your life, then you don't love them. If the only time you want to spend time with them is when their wearing apron, You don't love them, you only love their apron

In order for a marriage to be fruitful and lasting you must love your spouse when he or she is unclothed. We all have made mistakes, and we all are going to make more mistakes so don't despise one another scars. Scars are living testimonies of where God brought your from; therefore, expect for your spouse to make mistakes and don't act surprise when it happens. As long as we learn from our mistakes, then it was a mistake well made and purposed for us to grow. When a person gets naked, certain truths can be hard to swallow and every man and woman should understand that. Therefore, give thou spouse time to accept and digest the truth. It might not be easy at first. It takes time for wounds to heal. Remember love covers all sins, so putting a lot of love on top of the mistake you have made can ease their pain you cause them. Therefore, after each mistake, love them better, love them stronger and be consistent. Be ye tenderhearted, pitiful, forgiving one another like Christ has forgiven you.

When you're naked with each other, the relationship is free to blossom and it makes no difference what people think because thou knowest the truth. Those who know God, rejoiceth not in iniquity, but are happy with the truth, standing bold and confident in Christ, My Lord. Every soul needs a person they can be naked and not ashamed with. Someone you can uncover yourself to, because regardless of how much money you make or how good you dress, you can't hide the truth for long. For what's in darkness shall come to light. Therefore, it's important to be with someone who will love the truth about you. Your spouse should accept you as is, and appreciate what My Lord is creating thee to be. You should feel comfortable in raw form around him/her. You shouldn't have to put on any facade. You should be able to take all of your clothes off in front of him/her without fear, because your spouse should love you regardless if others approve or disapprove of it. Whatever weaknesses thou has, love is patient and thou shall wait on God in faith for growth and development. Therefore, the question is, can you **Love Me Naked**? Because if you can't **Love Me Naked** then you don't love **Me**.

TIRED OF LOVE

THEY THAT SOW IN TEARS SHALL REAP IN JOY. (PSALM 126:5)

If you want your relationship to work out, you cannot be the type of person that runs out on someone every time something goes wrong. Love doesn't require you to be a fool, but love does require you to be strong. You must have stamina to endure the storms and the growing pains of life with them. Neither you nor the person you love is perfect so mistakes will be made and sometimes those mistakes could be hurtful. Their attitude may not be sunny all their time, their actions may not be loving all the time, theirs words may not be nice all the time, their appearance may not be wonderful all the time, their odor may not be fresh all the time, their sex drive may not be high all the time and doing those down times more love is required of you. Understand you're not going to know how strong your love is for him or her until it's been tested and sometimes those test will come directly from them. What should you do when the person you have chosen to have and to hold in riches or poverty, sickness and health, till death do you part, makes it difficult for you to love them? What should you do when the commitment you made to love is being tried? The answer is simple. If you want your relationship to work you cannot get TIRED! You must remain steadfast in love. Understand God is using them to perfect his love in you, so although their acting up you're getting better. His strength is made perfect in weakness, so continue to love even when the same kind of good love you're giving them isn't been returned to you. If he or she is not doing right by you don't stop doing right by them. As long as you love them in deed and in truth he or she will never be able to use your actions as an excuse for their ill behavior towards you. You might shed many tears, but those tears are not in vain. God hears your request to change your spouse, but he is allowing things to happen because God is perfecting his love in you. Understand the greatest love is birthed

235

through suffering.

You must become perfect in love even as our Father in Heaven is perfect. As others often are, you cannot be "some timing" meaning, you can't only behave loving towards your spouse when he or she is being sweet to you, you must love them even when they're not loving you. You can't allow their unloving or dry attitude prevent you from walking in God's love. We are instructed to even love our enemies; therefore, when your spouse is acting as though he or she is your enemy, love them anyway. Continue to give your spouse the honor and respect although their not behaving worthy of it, knowing that God's love was given to you when you was walking unworthy of it. Although you might appear like a fool to many, it's called FAITH. Render good for their evil. Bless them when they curse you and pray for him or her if they're despitefully using you. Allow the wisdom of God to direct you on when to embrace and when to refrain from embracing. In many cases the more you love the more opposition you could initially face because the devil is going to work overtime fighting against your faith, but don't grow weary in well doing. God promises that those who sow in tears should reap in joy, if they faint not. Keep your eyes on the Lord, trust in him and one day you shall see your faithfulness rewarded and your joy shall come sevenfold in the time appointed.

LET US NOT BE WEARY IN WELL DOING: FOR IN DUE SEASON WE SHALL REAP IF WE FAINT NOT (Galatians 6;9)

If that man or woman suppose to be the LOVE of your life don't take their love for granted because when you behave unappreciative, unloving, ungrateful, careless, you're quenching their desire to love and do good by you. Why would a man continue to surprise you with gifts if you act like its nothing to you? Why should a woman continue to cook in her high heels and thongs if you act like you don't even see her when you come home? Don't let your reactions to their good actions be like water to their fire. If you're not treating her or him right not only are you putting their flame of love out, but you're making temptations harder for them to resist. Don't give the love of your life reasons not to love you, but do those things that add fuel to their fire. If love them right their love should always get stronger

LET US CONSIDER ONE ANOTHER TO PROVOKE UNTO LOVE AND GOOD WORKS (Hebrews 10:24)

Husband and wives your actions are powerful. They have the ability to make a person want to love you or they could cause a person to hate you. We are commanded to provoke love out of one another and the only way to accomplish that is by loving one another, so Men and women LOVE EACHOTHER. When you love your spouse he or she has no reason not to love you. When a person is behaving unaffectionate and hateful towards you, if you choose to behave as them, you surely aren't provoking them to treat you any better. If anything they'll feel as though they are justified in their wrongful actions. However, when you do right by them they'll look like a fool doing wrong by you because one good deed deserves another.

GLORY BE TO GOD

May this book, "Undivided Love," be a blessing to all that touch it. Hopefully it encourages singles to look forward to marriage and enlightens those who are already married. Married couples should be a sweet aroma to God. This book was inspired by the Spirit of God and written in simplicity to set the record straight on some issues that have been plaguing many marriages and keeping them from being that sweet-smelling mist. There is a time and place for every purpose under the sun and My Lord has saw fit to manifest this work during this hour to accomplish His purpose. My Lord has told me to tell His people to read the King James Version of the Gospel that has no commentary in it and to keep a Strong's Concordance at hand. All doctrines that are not congruent to the Word of God, trash it. Remember, you need not any man to teach you the Gospel, but the anointing that abiding in you shall teach you all things. Therefore, study to show thyself approved unto God that you may know the doctrine and whether it is of God. Submit to all truths and pursue peace with all men. May His Grace and Mercy be multiplied unto you through the knowledge of My Lord and Savior Jesus Christ.

For those who have read this book and have been in rebellion to the Word of God or do not know My Lord and Savior Jesus Christ and desire for Him to be Lord over their life please recite this prayer aloud:

Dear Father, I'm a sinner and I plead for your mercy. I do believe in my heart that your Son, Jesus Christ was crucified and rose again. I do believe that He died for the redemption of my soul and that His blood can wash my sins away. By no other name can I be saved, but by the name of your Son Jesus Christ. I repent and I ask you Lord to forgive me of all of my sins and let your Holy Spirit dwell within me. Please create in me a clean heart and let your will be done in My Life. In Jesus Name, Amen

Praise God for all those who have been touched by this revelation. Let the peace of God that passes all understanding rule in your hearts and minds. Be patient and steadfast in the faith. Enjoy this life and serve God in the Spirit, watch and pray always. Our God is powerful.

Thank you for thy support and be blessed!

Courtlandjr@aol.com

Sources

1. King James Bible

2. Strong's Concordance

3. Webster Dictionary

Made in the USA
Charleston, SC
16 July 2014